2026 FIRE HORSE YEAR FENG SHUI AND CHINESE ASTROLOGY PLANNER

MICHELE CASTLE

Welcome to the energies of the **Fire Horse in 2026!**

This year gallops in with passion, movement, and momentum, guided by the spirited and dynamic Fire Horse – a symbol of freedom, transformation, and unbridled ambition. The Horse is renowned for its independence, courage, and drive, embodying a restless quest for purpose and authenticity. With Fire as its ruling element, 2026 ignites enthusiasm, creativity, and a desire for bold action and change.

The **Fire Horse of 2026** brings a year charged with intensity and potential. It burns brightly with vitality, vision, and the power to break through limitations. This is a time when courage meets opportunity – a year that rewards those who dare to step forward, take calculated risks, and follow their inner calling. The Horse's fiery nature amplifies motivation and spontaneity, yet also calls for mindfulness and balance to prevent burnout or impulsive decisions.

In 2026, the Fire element dominates, symbolising passion, transformation, and illumination. Fire represents inspiration and visibility – it lights the path toward purpose, fame, and recognition. The Horse, aligned with the energy of movement and action, fuels ambition and innovation, making this a powerful year for launching new ventures, pursuing personal goals, and expressing your authentic self with confidence.

The **2026 Astrology & Feng Shui Planner** provides daily insights into your health, relationships, and business opportunities, offering practical guidance through Chinese Astrology, Flying Star, and the Bagua School. It's an empowering companion to help you harness the Fire Horse energy and ride its waves of transformation with clarity and direction.

Embrace the vibrant forces that 2026 brings:

- A year of passion, action, and dynamic growth.
- A time for courage, independence, and creative leadership.
- A period marked by transformation, visibility, and bold decisions.
- Expect rapid change, newfound freedom, and illuminating breakthroughs.

While Feng Shui doesn't promise miracles, understanding and wisely applying its principles helps harmonise your environment with the year's fiery rhythm. This ancient art allows you to balance action with calm, ensuring your energy flows in alignment with opportunity rather than chaos. Feng Shui – meaning *"wind and water"* – reminds us to move fluidly through change, grounded in wisdom and guided by purpose.

May **2026**, the Year of the Fire Horse, bring you **energy, inspiration, and fearless transformation** as you gallop toward your highest potential.

Published by Complete Feng Shui
Mb: 0421 116 799,
Email: info@completefengshui.com.au
Websites: www.completefengshui.com

2026 Feng Shui & Astrology Planner 2026 ©
Text copyright © Michele Castle   Illustrations copyright © Michele Castle

All rights reserved. No part of this publication may be reproduced, stored in a retrieval system or transmitted in any form or by any means, electronic, mechanical, photocopying, recording, or otherwise, without the prior written permission of Complete Feng Shui.

The author's moral right to be identified as the author of this book has been asserted.

Author: Michele Castle
Design copyright @completefengshui
Title: 2026 Feng Shui & Astrology Planner

ISBN: 978-1-7637996-5-3 (Hardcover)
ISBN: 978-1-7637996-6-0 (Paperback)
ISBN: 978-1-7637996-7-7 (EPUB)
December 2025

This Planner has been written to offer insight and planning for daily activities and energies in 2026, based on Flying Stars, Bagua, Chinese astrology, and date selection. The author, editor and publisher take no responsibility for the outcome of any information implemented from this planner.

This planner's information is summarised from the Chinese Thousand-Year Calendar and presented in a user-friendly format to help you enjoy prosperity throughout the year.

Vice President of the Association of Feng Shui Consultants (AFSC)
Platinum member of the Association of Feng Shui Consultants (AFSC)
Recognised as a Feng Shui training institution by the (AFSC)

facebook@completefengshui   instagram@completefengshui

Book Cover design, Book Layout & publishing assistance by manuscript2ebook.com

CONTENTS

Personal details viii
Resolutions for 2026 ix
2026 Year of Fire Horse 1
Chinese New Year Traditions 5
Auspicious Feng Shui Colours for 2026 7
How to Use the Chinese Zodiac Planner 9
Flying Star Feng Shui 10
Favourable Stars / Unfavourable Stars 11
2026 Flying Star Charts 12
2026 Afflictions 16
January 6 – February 3 is month of the Ox 18
January Flying Star 20
January Monthly Chinese Zodiac Overview 22
Chinese Zodiac Animal Relationships 26
February 4 – March 5 is month of the Tiger 30
February Flying Star 32
February Monthly Chinese Zodiac Overview 34
March 6 – April 4 is month of the Rabbit 40
March Flying Star 42
March Monthly Chinese Zodiac Overview 44
April 5 – May 5 is month of the Dragon 50
April Flying Star 52
April Monthly Chinese Zodiac Overview 54
The Feng Shui of Your Front Door 58
May 6 – June 5 is month of the Snake 62
May Flying Star 64
May Monthly Chinese Zodiac Overview 66
June 6 – July 6 is month of the Horse 72
June Flying Star 74

June Monthly Chinese Zodiac Overview 76

July 7 – August 7 is month of the Goat 82

July Flying Star 84

July Monthly Chinese Zodiac Overview 86

August 8 – September 7 is month of the Monkey 92

August Flying Star 94

August Monthly Chinese Zodiac Overview 96

Feng Shui Principles for the Bedroom 100

September 8 – October 7 is month of the Rooster 104

September Flying Star 106

September Monthly Chinese Zodiac Overview 108

Creating Zodiac Love Opportunities 112

October 8 – November 6 is month of the Dog 116

October Flying Star 118

October Monthly Chinese Zodiac Overview 120

November 7 – December 6 is month of the Pig 126

November Flying Star Forecast 128

November Monthly Chinese Zodiac Overview 130

December 7 – January 5 is month of the Rat 136

December Flying Star Forecast 138

December Monthly Chinese Zodiac Overview 140

Ideal Kitchen Placement in Feng Shui 144

January monthly 2027 Chinese Zodiac Overview 148

January 2027 Flying Star Forecast 150

Zodiac Secret Friends 152

Using Your Kua Number 154

Your Kua Number 158

Auspicious and Inauspicious directions based on your Kua Number 163

Calendar 2026 164

Calendar 2027 165

Year Planner 2026 166

WELCOME

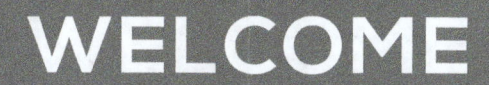

2026 A YEAR OF EXPANSION AND NEW POSSIBILITIES

Your Personal Information

Name ....

Date of Birth ....

Time of Birth ....

Animal Sign ....

Address ....
....
....

Telephone No. .... Office No. ....

Mobile No .... Fax No. ....

E-mail address ....

Favorite Websites ....
....

Secret Friend .... Allies ....

Conflict Animal ....

Peach Blossom Animal ....

Self-Element ....

Kua Number ....

Your House Facing Direction ....

Office Direction ....

Best Direction (Sheng Chi) .... Health Direction (Tien Yi) ....

Romance Direction (Nien Yen) .... Personal Growth Direction (Fu Wei).......

Unlucky (Ho Hai) .... Five Ghost (Wu Kwei) ....

Six Killings (Lui Sha) .... Total Loss (Chueh Ming) ....

Resolutions for 2026

....

....

....

....

....

....

....

....

....

....

....

....

....

As the Horse represents momentum and freedom, 2026 is the ideal year to shed what held you back, release outdated habits, and commit to personal transformation. The Fire Horse supports you in building confidence, expressing your true self, and stepping into leadership—whether in your career, relationships, health, or spiritual path.

This year reminds you that progress comes from movement. Even small steps, consistently made, create powerful change. The Fire Horse's energy brings visibility, recognition, and the strength to persevere, helping you turn goals into achievements and intentions into reality.

As you enter this vibrant new year, allow the Fire Horse to guide your resolutions with passion, purpose, and unstoppable vitality.

2026 YEAR OF THE FIRE HORSE

Bold, dynamic, and fiercely alive, the Year of the Fire Horse gallops into 2026 with unstoppable energy and transformative momentum. Unlike quieter, internal years, the Fire Horse thrives in open space, big decisions, and courageous leaps forward. This is a year ruled by passion, visibility, ambition, and the desire to break free from limitations.

Where the Snake of 2025 represented subtle transformation, 2026 brings **fast movement, vibrant change, and energetic ignition**. The Fire Horse's power is fuelled by dynamism, courage, and the willingness to move boldly in new directions.

The Spirit of the Fire Horse

The Horse has long been a symbol of freedom, ambition, power, and endurance in Chinese mythology. With the Fire element igniting its natural drive, the Horse becomes even more charismatic, expressive, and daring. Fire enhances action, confidence, brilliance, and leadership—making 2026 a year of reinvention, bold decisions, and increased desire for independence.

The Fire Horse encourages us to rise above stagnation, shake off anything that holds us back, and gallop toward aspirations with renewed determination. Its energy emboldens us to express our authentic selves, seek recognition for our accomplishments, and embrace opportunities that spark passion and purpose.

However, this fiery momentum must be balanced with grounding. In extremes, the Fire Horse may push toward impatience, impulsiveness, or burnout. This year calls for **bravery tempered by wisdom**, ensuring that bold action does not lead to unnecessary risks or conflict.

Energetic Themes of 2026

The Fire Horse radiates passion, intensity, and rapid acceleration. This energy encourages:

- Strong leadership and visibility
- Bold life changes
- Increased creativity and self-expression
- Rapid developments in career, finances, and relationships
- The release of old restraints
- Greater personal independence
- Heightened desire for exploration, movement, and freedom

Under this influence, 2026 becomes a year where growth occurs through action, forward motion, and decisive choices.

Zodiac Clashes in 2026

Clashing signs in 2026 include the **Rat, Ox, Rabbit, and Horse**. These signs may experience movement, surprise changes, and shifts in direction—similar to the "Travelling Horse" effect in BaZi.

Those affected may encounter:

- Travel or relocation
- Job transitions
- Relationship adjustments
- Sudden breakthroughs or endings
- A strong need to reset life direction

For these individuals, flexibility, patience, and emotional balance will be essential. Movement is not negative—it often opens new pathways that were previously impossible.

Duplicating Zodiac Year: Fire Horse Natives (1966, 2026)

For those born in a Horse year, 2026 becomes a **"Duplicating Zodiac Year"**, amplifying both strengths and weaknesses.

This means:

- Increased ambition and restlessness
- Higher desire for independence
- Greater boldness in decision-making
- Strong urge to change career, lifestyle, or relationships
- Potential for impulsiveness or conflict if emotions run hot

Caution is advised in health, finances, and interpersonal dynamics. While the year brings immense growth potential, grounding strategies and mindful choices will prevent unnecessary upheaval.

Navigating Fire Horse Challenges

The Fire Horse year burns bright—sometimes too bright. Hidden tensions can arise from miscommunication, impatience, overcommitment, or emotional reactivity.

The Horse's energy teaches:

- Pause before reacting
- Choose clarity over speed
- Avoid emotional impulsiveness
- Maintain protection around finances

- Balance ambition with personal well-being

Like the spirited Horse, challenges can be managed gracefully when met with calm, awareness, and strategic movement.

Comparison to 2025 Wood Snake

Where 2025 focused on subtle growth, internal reflection, and quiet strategy, **2026 flips the dynamic entirely.**

In contrast:

- 2025 was introspective; 2026 is expressive
- 2025 required patience; 2026 rewards decisive action
- 2025 nurtured wisdom; 2026 demands bravery
- 2025 brought slow progress; 2026 brings fast breakthroughs

The Fire Horse invites liberation, visibility, and a readiness to leap into new opportunities with confidence and enthusiasm.

Love & Relationships in 2026

Relationships become more passionate, expressive, and emotionally charged under the Fire Horse's influence.

This year encourages:

- Bold declarations of love
- Reigniting passion in existing relationships
- Greater need for independence
- Fiery attraction and strong chemistry
- Quick developments in romance—both good and challenging

Singles may find love suddenly and unexpectedly, often with someone vibrant, confident, or inspiring.

Couples may need to balance passion with patience. Communication is key, as misunderstandings or emotional reactions may flare more quickly. Relationships built on trust, respect, and mutual support will grow stronger, while those already strained may face essential turning points.

Career & Finances in 2026

2026 is a powerful year for professional advancement, visibility, and leadership.

The Fire Horse supports:

- Career breakthroughs
- Public recognition
- Entrepreneurship and bold new ventures

- Creative industries, media, marketing, performance
- Jobs requiring speed, decision-making, and innovation

This is not a year for hesitation. Well-timed action leads to meaningful success.

Financially, the year brings opportunities but also volatility. Thoughtful planning, strategic risk-taking, and grounded financial decisions will be essential. Avoid impulsive spending or overly risky investments.

Global Themes in the Fire Horse Year

On a worldwide level, 2026 may bring:

- Bold political moves and leadership changes
- Strong public movements and demands for freedom
- Rapid advancements in technology and innovation
- Heightened global visibility and media influence
- Increases in travel, mobility, and global interactions
- Social tension or conflict if emotions run high

Diplomacy, patience, and strategic cooperation will be essential to balance this fiery global energy.

The Essence of 2026 – A Year of Bold Transformation

The Fire Horse brings a year of high energy, courageous choices, and rapid transformation. This is not a time for standing still. Success comes through momentum, self-belief, and daring to take the reins of your life.

Where the Snake transformed silently from within, the Horse transforms loudly, visibly, and through action.

2026 is a year to:

- Step into leadership
- Pursue dreams with passion
- Break free from limiting situations
- Honour your individuality
- Embrace new challenges
- Move boldly toward the future

Those who align with the Fire Horse's vibrant, unstoppable energy will find themselves riding into a year filled with opportunity, success, and exhilarating new beginnings.

CHINESE NEW YEAR TRADITIONS

Key Practices:

Thoroughly clean your home, removing all clutter.

Keep old brooms and brushes away and replace them with new ones to avert bad luck.

Settle existing debts if possible.

Reconcile any conflicts with family, friends, neighbours, and business partners.

Preparations, Customs, and Superstitions:

Use fresh red envelopes (ang pows) and new banknotes. Stock up on Mandarin oranges.

Display a circular candy tray.

Decorate with flowers like plum blossom, peach blossom, and pussy willow, symbolising happiness and good fortune. Wear new clothes and shoes for the occasion.

Lunar Chinese New Year Etiquette:

Greet others with "Gong Xi Fa Cai" to wish them a prosperous New Year.

Prepare food in advance to avoid using sharp tools on New Year's Day to preserve luck.

Maintain a positive, joyful atmosphere, refraining from negative expressions.

Avoid washing your hair on the first day of the New Year, as it's associated with washing away prosperity.

Stick to bright, auspicious colours like red and gold while avoiding white and black.

Exchange Mandarin oranges when visiting, and unmarried individuals receive Hong Baos (Ang POWS) for good luck.

Embracing Lunar Chinese New Year's Significance

Chinese New Year, Lunar Day 1, 2026, falling on 17 February, is a pivotal moment in Chinese culture. The belief is that initiating the year with precise actions, timing, and direction can invite good fortune and prosperity for the year ahead. The tradition involves selecting a specific direction to welcome auspicious stars through prayer offerings from 3:00 AM to 6:59 AM. These stars are aligned with distinct purposes: Wealth resides in the South, the South is for Happiness, the East symbolises Nobility and Patronage, and the Southeast is the doorway to Good Luck. This practice reflects the' rich tapestry of Chinese customs and their deep-rooted connection to auspicious beginnings.

UNVEILING THE CLASH IN 2026

Chinese astrology identifies four Zodiac signs that clash with the Annual Ruling Sign each year. In 2026, these clashing signs are the Rooster, Horse, Rabbit and Rat, collectively known as "Treasure Boxes" in this realm. The severity of these clashes varies depending on an individual's Ba Zi chart. The impact can be more pronounced if two or more Clashing signs are present. The Rat sign faces the most significant challenge due to a direct clash with the Horse sign, which can introduce changes or obstacles. Individuals with these signs should maintain a low profile, exercise caution, and avoid impulsive decisions to mitigate potential negative consequences, including accidents, conflicts, scandals, health issues, divorce, or financial setbacks.

DECODING THE SIGNIFICANCE OF THE 2026 CLASHES

In 2026, different Chinese Zodiac signs face various types of clashes, each with its recommended resolutions:

For the Rooster, it's a clash of interests; the key is maintaining humility and avoiding conflicts.

The Rat experiences a direct clash and should opt for a low-profile approach, steering clear of adventure, rule-breaking, and prioritising personal safety.

If you're a Horse, you encounter an offending clash, making it vital to stay low-key and avoid confrontations and rule-breaking while focusing on personal well-being.

Those born under the Rabbit sign face a penalty clash that requires self-discipline, flexibility, and vigilance against betrayal.

DISCOVERING THE MOST COMPATIBLE SIGN IN 2026

Each year, one of the 12 zodiac signs aligns harmoniously with the ruling zodiac sign, often referred to as "The Grand Duke" or Tai Shui. In 2026, the Goat sign claims this favourable position. Per ancient beliefs, carrying a Goat emblem or symbol can help ward off potential metaphysical ill effects and foster greater harmony and positive energy in your everyday life.

Secret Friends for Your Aid

Secret Friends —zodiac signs that provide support and compatibility —can help counter the metaphysical challenges posed by clashes with the Grand Duke. They are also believed to attract helpful and supportive individuals into your life. The Secret Friend pairings for the Chinese Lunar Zodiac signs are as follows:

Rat: Ox, Dragon, Monkey　　**Ox:** Rat, Snake, Rooster　　**Tiger:** Pig, Dog, Horse

Rabbit: Dog, Pig, Goat　　**Dragon:** Rooster, Monkey, Rat　　**Snake:** Monkey, Rooster, Ox

Horse: Goat, Tiger, Dog　　**Goat:** Horse, Rabbit, Pig　　**Monkey:** Rat, Dragon, Snake

Rooster: Snake, Ox, Dragon　　**Dog:** Rabbit, Horse, Tiger　　**Pig:** Tiger, Goat, Rabbit

AUSPICIOUS FENG SHUI COLOURS FOR 2026

The Year of the Yang Fire Horse brings fast, bright, and unmistakable energy. It is a year of movement, courage, visibility, and bold choices. In Feng Shui, colour becomes one of the easiest ways to ride this fiery momentum without letting it burn out of control. The right tones help you harness passion and drive while keeping your emotions and energy field balanced.

At the heart of 2026 is Yang Fire, the dominant force of the Fire Horse. A clear, intense vermilion red symbolises this—the key empowering colour of the year. Vermilion represents vitality, recognition, and enthusiasm. It's perfect for moments when you need to stand out, be heard, or lead: an important meeting, a presentation, a launch, a first date, or any situation where you want your presence remembered. You don't need to drape yourself in red from head to toe; a scarf, lipstick, bracelet, tie, bag, or planner cover in this shade is enough to "switch on" the Fire Horse frequency.

Because the Fire element is so strong in 2026, it also needs soothing and stabilising companions. Soft sky or horizon blues carry the Water element, cooling the intensity of Fire and helping with clear communication, negotiation, and emotional ease. Fresh leaf and meadow greens bring in Wood, supporting growth, healing, learning, and adjusting to new beginnings. Warm golden yellows and gentle earthy tones (sand, maize, light tan) link to Earth, grounding the year's fast pace and helping with focus, organisation, and practical decisions. Delicate metallics—antique gold, champagne, bronze—add the Metal element, supporting fairness, structure, and discernment.

Feng Shui always works with both the 5 Elements and the annual Flying Stars, which means there is no single "magic colour" for every room and every person. Each home has its own energy map, and each individual has their own elemental make-up. As a general principle for 2026, let vermilion red be your activator and use blue, green, yellow, earth and metal tones as your stabilisers. Rotate them according to what you need that day: more red when you want courage and visibility, more blue and green when you need calm and clarity, more earth and metal tones when you're dealing with money, contracts, or long-term plans.

These colours work best when they move with you rather than sitting forgotten in a corner. Clothing, jewellery, handbags, phone covers, diary covers, water bottles, and even a small coloured ribbon or bookmark are all simple ways to keep aligned with the energies of the Fire Horse year. Think subtle, conscious touches rather than overwhelming blocks of colour.

From an elemental point of view, fiery and dynamic signs such as Horse, Tiger, Dragon, Dog, Rooster, Monkey and Goat generally cope well with the intensity of

2026 and can embrace vermilion more boldly. Water-sensitive signs like Rat and Pig often feel the heat more quickly and respond better to cooling blues and grounding earth colours, using red in small accents. Metal or more reserved signs, like Ox, Rabbit, Snake and Rooster, may find that soft greens, gentle yellows and metallic shades help them stay centred while still enjoying the year's excitement.

In the Year of the Yang Fire Horse, colours become more than fashion or decoration—they act as daily energetic tools. Choosing what you wear and surrounding yourself with becomes a quiet ritual of intention. Used wisely, the 2026 palette helps you express your true self, protect your energy, and channel this powerful Fire Horse year into growth, love, success and inspired action, rather than stress or burnout.

How to use the Chinese Zodiac Planner

Clarity and good timing are vital in ensuring that whatever you undertake is given the best possible chance of success. Even simple everyday activities can have substantial adverse outcomes if riddled with obstacles and bad energy.

ACTIVITY ICONS  travelling, moving, renovating, or signing a contract

This planner contains specially calculated auspicious dates for significant activities like cutting your hair, celebrations, travelling, moving, renovating or breaking ground, or signing a contract. Icons on each page mark these.

Understanding The Icons

FAVOURABLE DAYS FOR SPECIFIC TASKS

The icons on each page reveal favourable days for travelling, love and relationship luck, moving house, signing contracts, cutting your hair, buying a car, celebrating, meeting people, starting construction and renovating.

Unfavourable days are also indicated for any significant activities on clash days.

CHINESE ASTROLOGY ANIMALS

Each day's summary includes good /bad days for certain animal signs. When undertaking any significant activity, always check whether it is a good/bad day for your sign, as this overrides whatever the icons indicate. If it is a bad day for the Horse, then all activities will NOT be promising for the Horse that day, no matter what the icons indicate. The Horse must avoid scheduling important issues that day.

FLYING STAR FENG SHUI

Getting your Feng Shui right for the coming year and energising the promising sectors in 2026 will help ensure smooth sailing and a prosperous year ahead.

As we move from one year to the next, energy changes. Transforming from Yin to Yang, from element to element, from one animal sign to the next. Depending on the ruling element and animal, the energy in the home and its occupants also changes from one month to the next. Time exerts a powerful impact on your Feng Shui, luck, and destiny.

Good Feng Shui cannot and does not last forever. It must be recharged with small but significant changes every year. Energy must be refreshed, reorganised and re-energised. Spaces and places need rejuvenation. Energy must be kept moving.

The Flying Stars formula of Feng Shui is a technical approach that directly addresses the effect of time on the energy of homes and businesses and holds a beautiful promise that enables you to improve your luck tremendously. The 2026 Feng Shui chart maps out the distribution of energy in each of the eight sectors of the compass, as well as the centre.

The best strategy is to take care of the negative Stars first and then concentrate on boosting the good ones. Pay closer attention to the sectors where your main door, living room and bedrooms are located. The luck in the main entrance and living room sector affects everyone in the household, while the bedroom alters the fate of those who sleep in it.

The Flying Star energy undergoes annual changes, and a dominant star positioned at the centre of the Lo Shu chart governs the overall energy for the year. In 2026, the reigning Flying Star is the 1, while different stars influence specific sectors. For instance, the West is impacted by the Flying Star 3, the NE by the Flying Star 4, and so on. Additionally, the Flying Stars' energy varies monthly as a new star joins the annual stars, influencing each month's energy. You can find a monthly overview at the start of each month. Furthermore, a daily Flying Star number reflects the energy of the day. Understanding the meaning and energy of the Flying Stars allows you to assess the daily quality of luck.

FAVOURABLE STARS

1 Victory Triumph and Success Star (**Water Element**): Helps attain victory over competition and enhances career promotion and monetary growth. Strengthen and improve energy by placing a Victory Horse, Ruyi, or Dragon Tortoise. A water feature would also be incredibly beneficial.

2 Rebirth and Positive Change (**Earth Element**): This Star supports health growth and well-being, bringing improvement to physical ailments and diseases... Support the energy by placing a Wu Lou (Health Gourd), Six Gold Coins on a red tassel, a Saltwater Cure and a Quan Yin in the Southwest.

4 Romance and Literacy Star (Wood Element): Good Star improves relationship opportunities, study, and literary fortune for writers and scholars. Enhance luck with bright lights, fire energy, and wood energy: Place Mandarin Ducks or Huggers, peach blossom animals, plants and fresh flowers in this area.

6 Heavenly Luck Star (Metal Element): Associated with good fortune and help from heaven, it brings speculative luck, power, and authority. Use bright lights, a water feature and Metal to enhance, such as Six Gold Coins on red tassels and Gold Ingots within this area. A Horse will also assist.

8 Retired Prosperity Star (Earth Element): Signifies steady wealth, prosperity, success and happiness. Strengthen and enhance by placing any form of wealth symbolism such as a Buddha, Wealth God, Six Gold Coins on a red tassel, and Gold Ingots.

9 Multiplying Current Prosperity Star (Fire Element): Signifies future prosperity; spurs celebrations, festivities, gatherings and excellent good luck. Enhance with red accessories, bright lights, or any wealth symbolism such as a Buddha, a Wealth God, 9 Gold Coins on a red tassel, or Gold Ingots.

UNFAVOURABLE STARS

3 Hostile, Conflict and Dispute Star (Wood Element): An evil Star signifies lawsuits, hostility and quarrels. Brings misunderstandings among staff, clients and colleagues and trouble with the authorities. I recommend placing Fire energy in this area, such as bright lights or a red piece of paper, or you can use any red décor object. If your front door is in this area, I recommend placing Temple Lions and the Evil Eye symbol. Remove any excess water or plants. Remove Metal windchimes. Do not overstimulate with radio or TV energy.

5 Misfortune and Obstacles Star (Earth Element), also known as Wu Wang or 5 Yellow Star: It is considered the most vicious and dangerous of the nine Stars; it brings all kinds of misfortunes, accidents, losses and death. Subdue with a Brass 5-element Pagoda and a Saltwater Cure in the centre. A Ganesha will also assist with the removal of obstacles. Keep electrical equipment to a minimum and avoid the colours red and yellow. Try to avoid any significant activity within this sector.

7 Robbery and Evil Star (Metal Element): This unlucky star brings loss, robbery, violence, and gossip to the West sector. Suppress by placing three pieces of Lucky Bamboo in a vase of water and bright lights in this area, along with the Evil Eye Symbol, one Blue Rhinoceros and one Blue Elephant, or two Blue Rhinoceroses for extra protection. If your front door is located here, I also recommend Temple Lions.

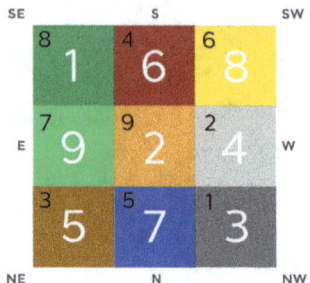
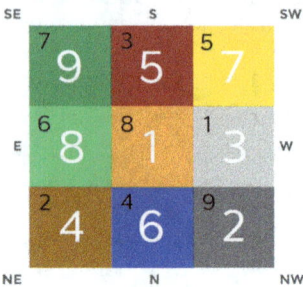
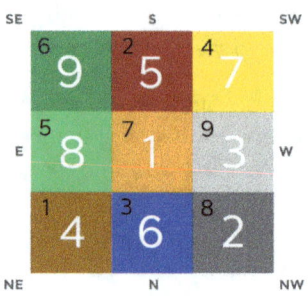
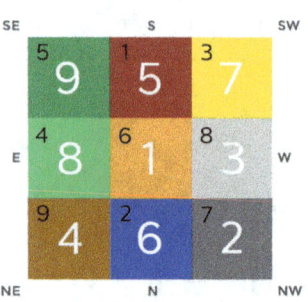
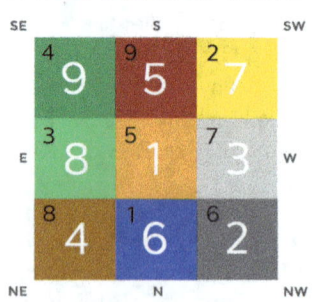
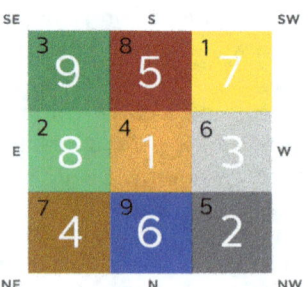
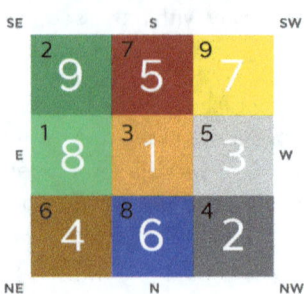
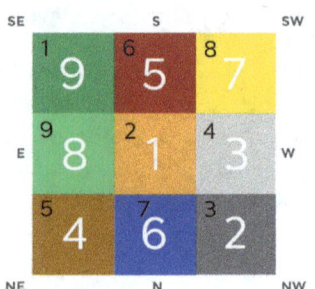

SEPTEMBER 2026

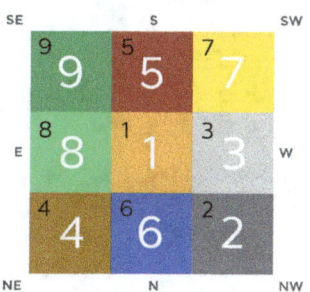

OCTOBER 2026

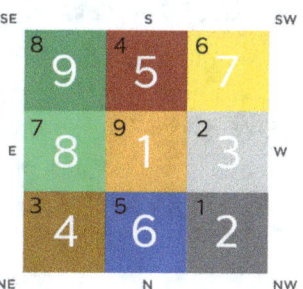

NOVEMBER 2026

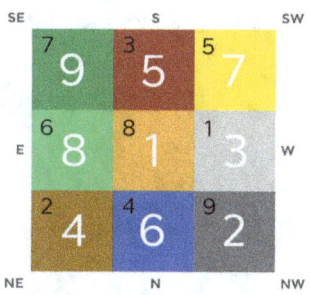

DECEMBER 2026

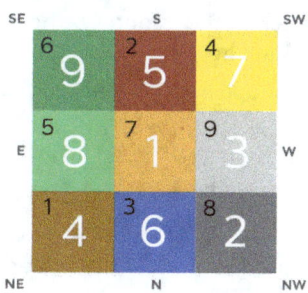

JANUARY 2027

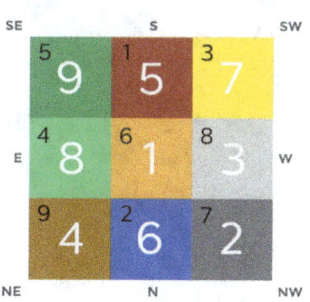

ANNUAL 2026

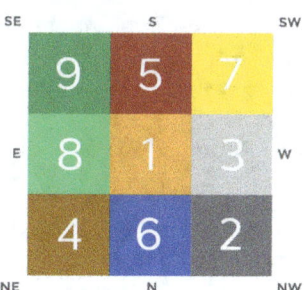

2026 Chinese Astrology Planner 13

Legend of the 12 Zodiac Animals

The Great Race of Time, Spirit, and Destiny

Long ago, when Heaven and Earth were still in harmony and the balance of yin and yang danced perfectly in rhythm, the Jade Emperor decided to create a way to measure the cycles of time.

He called upon all the animals of the kingdom to take part in a grand race – across rivers, valleys, and mountains – and declared that the first twelve to reach the celestial gates would be honoured with a place in the zodiac, ruling over the destiny of humankind.

The Clever Rat

The smallest of them all, the Rat was not the fastest – but he was clever. Riding silently on the back of the strong Ox, he waited until the very last moment to leap forward, crossing the finish line first.

Thus, the Rat claimed the first year, teaching us that wit, timing, and intelligence often triumph over size or strength.

The Steadfast Ox

Second came the humble Ox, who carried the Rat without complaint. Patient, steady, and devoted, he shows that persistence and hard work bring success. The Ox reminds us that the journey is not about competition – it's about purpose.

The Brave Tiger

Third was the fierce Tiger, whose courage and willpower roared across the finish line. Though the current was strong, his heart was stronger. The Tiger symbolises bravery and the unshakable spirit that faces challenges head-on.

The Gentle Rabbit

The graceful Rabbit bounded from stone to stone, elegant and careful, but was swept by a sudden wave – only to land safely on a floating log. Luck was on her side. Her presence in the zodiac reminds us that faith and serenity can guide us when control cannot.

The Noble Dragon

The Dragon could have easily won the race – his power was unmatched. Yet, seeing the drought below, he stopped to bring rain to the suffering lands. Arriving fifth, the Dragon's compassion and integrity shine brighter than his strength.

The Wise Snake

The Snake glided quietly behind the Horse, unseen but constantly aware. At the final stretch, he startled the Horse with a flick of his tail and slipped ahead. The Snake's wisdom lies in stillness and strategy – seeing what others overlook.

The Free-Spirited Horse

The Horse galloped with passion and speed, her mane flowing like fire in the wind. Though startled into seventh place, her energy and freedom became her gift. The Horse reminds us to live fully, to run wild, and to follow the rhythm of our spirit.

The Peaceful Goat

The Goat, alongside the Monkey and Rooster, built a raft to cross the river together. Her kindness and teamwork won her the eighth spot. The Goat teaches harmony and the strength of gentle cooperation.

The Inventive Monkey

Clever and curious, the Monkey's mind was his magic. He saw opportunity where others saw obstacles, and he swung into ninth place. His creativity shows us that the path of play and innovation leads to joy and success.

The Proud Rooster

The Rooster crowed at dawn, guiding the raft's journey with confidence and clarity. His sense of duty placed him tenth — a symbol of pride, order, and the power of leading by example.

The Loyal Dog

The Dog was strong and capable, but delayed his arrival because he couldn't resist bathing in the river's refreshing water. His eleventh place was earned with laughter and loyalty. The Dog represents faithfulness, love, and the joy of living in the moment.

The Easygoing Pig

Last came the Pig, who had stopped for a meal and a nap along the way. When she finally crossed the line, she did so with a happy heart and full belly. The Pig's place reminds us that contentment and simplicity are forms of abundance, too.

The Eternal Cycle

And so the Jade Emperor smiled, for each animal had revealed the essence of life's outstanding balance — intelligence, perseverance, courage, grace, compassion, wisdom, freedom, kindness, creativity, confidence, loyalty, and joy.

From that day forward, each year would carry the spirit of one of these twelve animals, weaving their qualities into the lives and destinies of humankind — a sacred rhythm of time and transformation that continues to this day.

2026 AFFLICTIONS

In 2026, the South (172.5 - 187.5) will be the designated location of the Tai Sui, also known as the Grand Duke, for the year. The Grand Duke is considered a celestial entity deserving of respect and should not be disturbed or confronted. Significant renovations or earthmoving in this sector are highly recommended to be avoided throughout the year and to maintain a sense of tranquillity in this area. Placing a Chi Lin, Pi Yao, and Fu Dog in the South, facing the North, can help appease and harmonise this sector, but it's best to avoid disturbances altogether.

In Chinese astrology, Tai Sui, or the Grand Duke of Jupiter, is a powerful energy that must be respected and not confronted. Disturbing Tai Sui can bring misfortunes ranging from career setbacks to health issues and financial loss. Grand Master believes that "The Grand Duke can cause havoc, and you will feel the impact" if offended.

Tai Sui's location changes annually; in 2026, it resides in the South (172.5° - 187.5°). To avoid conflict with Tai Sui, it's crucial not to face this direction or undertake significant renovations or earthmoving activities in this sector. To harmonise the energy, you can place protective Feng Shui items facing the North, like a Chi Lin, Pi Yao, or Fu Dog in the South. However, the best approach is to avoid disturbing this area altogether.

In 2026, the North will be influenced by the presence of the Three Killings, a challenging energy that can cause health issues and conflicts if disturbed. To minimise its negative impact, it is advised not to sit with your back to the North; instead, face this direction while keeping your back toward the South. Major renovations or earthmoving activities in the North should be avoided to maintain a harmonious atmosphere.

To neutralise the effects of the Three Killings, a common remedy is to place a set of Three Celestial Guardians—such as the Qilin, Fu Dog, and Pi Xiu—in the North sector of your home or workplace. Additionally, lighting up this area with a bright lamp or hanging a metal wind chime can further help to diminish the energy. However, the best approach is to avoid disturbing this sector altogether.

In 2026, the South will be influenced by The Five Yellow Star or Wu Wang, which is one of the most harmful Feng Shui afflictions, bringing severe illness, financial loss, and obstacles to success. As an Earth element affliction, its location changes annually, occupying 45 degrees of the compass. To avoid activating its adverse effects, it is advised to refrain from renovations, digging, or cutting trees in the affected sector. Loud noises, pets, and frequent activity should be minimised. Dim lighting can help appease the energy, especially in areas like the main entrance or bedroom.

January 6 – February 3 is the Month of the Ox

Ox Chinese Horoscope 2025: Navigating Challenges and Opportunities

Ox Birth Years: 1925, 1937, 1949, 1961, 1973, 1985, 1997, 2009, 2021, 2033

OX – A Year of Growth, Vitality, and Reward in the Fire Horse Cycle

2026 promises to be an eventful and empowering year for those born under the dependable and steadfast sign of the Ox. After a period of consolidation and endurance, the energetic and adventurous Yang Fire Horse rides in to awaken fresh momentum and illuminate new paths. Metaphysically, this year carries a stronger, healthier current for the Ox, with auspicious Celestial Stars offering protection, support, and new benefactors. You are surrounded by helpful people and circumstances that keep you safe, grounded, and moving forward with confidence.

Career & Opportunities

Professionally, this is a year of expansion, recognition, and advancement. The Fire Horse's yang energy ignites ambition, courage, and leadership—qualities that combine beautifully with your practical and disciplined Ox nature. You may find yourself drawn to new projects or business opportunities that stretch your comfort zone yet promise long-term growth.

Those in management or business ownership will experience favourable winds for expansion, rebranding, or diversification, while employees may see promotions, new responsibilities, or greater visibility.

The key to your success lies in openness—be willing to try innovative approaches and embrace creative collaboration. With the right balance of persistence and flexibility, the Fire Horse will carry your professional goals to new heights.

Tip: Step outside your usual rhythm. Say yes to fresh ideas, and trust that change now leads to lasting reward.

Wealth & Prosperity

Financially, 2026 is a promising and potentially lucrative year. All the hard work and long hours you've invested in previous cycles begin to pay off, delivering steady profits, new income streams, and solid financial returns.

The Fire Horse stimulates boldness in investment and spending, but your innate caution will protect you from impulsive choices. Use this year's energy to restructure finances, upgrade systems, or reinvest profits into sustainable ventures.

Opportunities for international trade, travel-linked business, or collaborations abroad may also appear.

Tip: Prosperity expands when you take calculated, inspired risks. Back your intuition with strategy and act while the flame burns bright.

Love & Relationships

Romance blooms under the influence of the Fire Horse, and Ox individuals can look forward to greater warmth and excitement in their personal lives. For singles, this is an ideal year to meet someone new or deepen a budding connection—primarily through travel, social events, or professional networks.

For those already in relationships, passion and playfulness return, inviting you to reignite the spark and strengthen emotional intimacy. However, with the fiery energy of the Horse in play, patience and communication are essential—avoid stubbornness and learn to flow with change rather than resist it.

Tip: Open your heart to spontaneity. Love flourishes when you balance loyalty with a touch of adventure.

Health & Well-being

The Ox is typically robust and resilient, but the fast-paced Fire Horse energy may tempt you into overworking, overindulging, or pushing physical limits. While no major illnesses are indicated, maintaining balance is crucial.

Nourish your body with grounding routines, wholesome food, and sufficient rest. Prioritise movement and circulation—yoga, walking, swimming, or outdoor exercise will harmonise your energy.

Tip: Listen to your body. Regular self-care ensures you can harness the Fire Horse's vitality without burning out.

Symbolism of the Ox and Fire Horse

- The Ox symbolises strength, endurance, and reliability. It represents perseverance through steady effort and the slow accumulation of success.

- The Fire Horse symbolises passion, speed, transformation, and unbridled freedom. Its energy blazes with creativity, courage, and the drive to explore new frontiers.

Together, this pairing of Earth and Fire elements creates a year where patience meets passion, and discipline dances with dynamism. You're invited to merge your steadfast nature with the Horse's fire—to move forward boldly yet wisely.

Final Overview Tip for 2026

This is your year to build upon strong foundations while embracing innovation and connection. The Fire Horse urges you to release rigidity and trust movement—to let inspiration guide your hard work. Stay grounded in your values, but allow passion and possibility to lead. When strength meets spark, success is inevitable.

JANUARY Flying Star 9: Abundant Prosperity and Beyond

January starts the year and rejoices under the luminous influence of Flying Star 9, a radiant beacon in the celestial tapestry. Known as the Star of Current Prosperity, this star shines brilliantly over completion, fame, celebration, wealth, intelligence, popularity, happiness, and acclaim. As a dynamic Fire Star, its vibrant energy sparks a cascade of joyous gatherings and festive occasions, inviting all to bask in its auspicious glow. Dubbed the "Star of Completion," Flying Star 9 brings projects and endeavours to their triumphant conclusion, nurturing financial success and prosperity.

This star is a powerful catalyst for both present and future ventures, magnifying the means of abundance and ensuring that the seeds of effort previously sown bear fruit. Its influence is particularly potent, as Flying Star 9 illuminates their paths with its brilliant energy. Those aligned with this star, especially the eldest daughter and those born under the Dragon and Snake zodiacs, are encouraged to embrace challenges enthusiastically, knowing victory is within reach.

As the ultimate harbinger of prosperity, Flying Star 9 accelerates wealth accumulation, boosts business profits, and enhances investments. It also elevates fame and recognition, casting a celestial spotlight on those pursuing success in various fields. In the current cosmic configuration, Flying Star 9 is the most potent force among the divine energies, making engaging with spaces influenced by it highly beneficial. Whether embarking on new business ventures, planning a wedding, or starting a family, the energy of Flying Star 9 offers a powerful boost to these life-changing endeavours.

To amplify its auspicious energy, incorporate wealth-enhancing symbols into your surroundings. Consider placing a wealth jar, a trio of horses, or Buddha figurines in prominent positions. Arranging 9 Gold Coins on a tassel or displaying a Wealth God figure and Gold Ingots further strengthens the star's influence. Multiples of nine, vibrant lighting, and red-themed decor—such as red phoenix symbols, upholstery, and accessories—elevate the energy even more. For an extra touch of prosperity, introduce a water feature with nine fish to amplify the flow of abundance.

Flying Star 9 emerges as a radiant symbol of prosperity and joy, guiding all who embrace its effervescent energy toward a bountiful journey ahead.

In January, the East sector of the Luo Shu or Bagua School of Feng Shui will be graced by the annual Flying Star 9. This sector, deeply associated with health, longevity, and overall well-being, provides a prime opportunity to enhance these vital aspects of life.

The Wood element governs the East, and incorporating both Wood and Water elements can amplify its positive influence on health and vitality. One practical remedy is to place bamboo in a water feature, as this combination strengthens the Wood element and supports a flourishing state of health. Introducing greenery, plants, and vibrant flowers will further invigorate this sector. The East is also home to the celestial Green Dragon, a symbol of auspicious fortune. Positioning a dragon figurine in this area can optimise the family's luck and overall well-being. Consider placing a Quan Yin statue to safeguard and nurture your physical and emotional vitality, enhancing your protection and health.

Refer to page 12 for this month flying star chart

01 | JANUARY 2026

The Fire Horse Year

1 Thursday
Animal: **Wood Pig**
Flying Star: **3**
Good Day: **Tiger**
Bad Day: **Snake**

2 Friday
Animal: **Fire Rat**
Flying Star: **4**
Good Day: **Ox**
Bad Day: **Horse**

3 Saturday
Animal: **Fire Ox**
Flying Star: **5**
Good Day: **Rat**
Bad Day: **Goat**

4 Sunday
Animal: **Earth Tiger**
Flying Star: **6**
Good Day: **Pig**
Bad Day: **Monkey**

5 Monday
Animal: **Earth Rabbit**
Flying Star: **7**
Good Day: **Dog**
Bad Day: **Rooster**

6 Tuesday
Animal: **Metal Dragon**
Flying Star: **8**
Good Day: **Rooster**
Bad Day: **Dog**

7 Wednesday
Animal: **Metal Snake**
Flying Star: **9**
Good Day: **Monkey**
Bad Day: **Pig**

JANUARY MONTHLY 2026 CHINESE ZODIAC OVERVIEW

RAT

The past year may have presented challenges, yet it ultimately supported your growth and resilience. As you step into the energetic Yang Fire Horse year – a year that naturally clashes with your sign – focus on staying balanced and prepared. Careful planning, emotional steadiness, and a positive outlook will help you transform potential tension into strength. Keep your goals clear and move mindfully toward a stable, productive year ahead.

OX

After a year of ups and downs, you emerge wiser and stronger. Though recent months may have tested your patience, they have also refined your perseverance. As you welcome the dynamic energy of the Fire Horse year, take time to realign your vision and set new intentions. Let joy and renewed enthusiasm guide your path – this is your moment to build on past achievements and invite prosperity into your next chapter.

TIGER

You are entering the Yang Fire Horse year with renewed excitement and readiness for action. The lessons of the past year have strengthened your confidence, preparing you to ride this powerful energy with courage and purpose. Positive developments are on the horizon – both personally and professionally. Maintain goodwill and strong relationships with colleagues and allies; teamwork and generosity will magnify your success.

RABBIT

The trials of the previous year have shaped your wisdom and grace. Now, as you transition into the vibrant Fire Horse year, soothing and supportive energy helps you find your footing again. With renewed clarity and a deeper understanding of your goals, this is the ideal time to move forward with optimism. Stay open-hearted and let positivity guide your actions – the year ahead holds promise and growth.

DRAGON

After a fulfilling and eventful year, you step into 2026 with confidence and purpose. January's energy is bright, bringing new opportunities for wealth and expansion. As you prepare to welcome the bold influence of the Fire Horse, take time to refine your plans and focus on meaningful goals. Strategic action now will set the foundation for an abundant and empowering year ahead.

SNAKE

As momentum builds, optimism and renewed enthusiasm flow into your world. The Fire Horse year supports your ambitions and opens doors to new ventures. Projects or business plans initiated now are well-favoured and likely to progress smoothly.

01 | JANUARY 2026

The Fire Horse Year

8 Thursday
Animal: **Water Horse**
Flying Star: **1**
Good Day: **Goat**
Bad Day: **Rat**

9 Friday
Animal: **Water Goat**
Flying Star: **2**
Good Day: **Horse**
Bad Day: **Ox**

10 Saturday
Animal: **Wood Monkey**
Flying Star: **3**
Good Day: **Snake**
Bad Day: **Tiger**

11 Sunday
Animal: **Wood Rooster**
Flying Star: **4**
Good Day: **Dragon**
Bad Day: **Rabbit**

12 Monday
Animal: **Fire Dog**
Flying Star: **5**
Good Day: **Rabbit**
Bad Day: **Dragon**

13 Tuesday
Animal: **Fire Pig**
Flying Star: **6**
Good Day: **Tiger**
Bad Day: **Snake**

14 Wednesday
Animal: **Earth Rat**
Flying Star: **7**
Good Day: **Ox**
Bad Day: **Horse**

Trust your instincts and maintain steady discipline – your efforts this month will set a prosperous tone for the months to follow.

HORSE

After an eventful and transformative year, you now stand at the threshold of your own ruling cycle – the powerful Yang Fire Horse year. January brings fulfilment, gratitude, and joy as you reflect on how far you've come. Embrace the lessons of the past while celebrating your progress. The energy ahead is dynamic and full of opportunity – ride it with confidence and clarity of purpose.

GOAT

If you've used the past year for growth and reflection, this month brings deep satisfaction and renewal. The Fire Horse year welcomes you with optimism and strong support from lucky stars. Financial energy looks promising, and expansion opportunities abound. Take time to nurture your well-being and celebrate how far you've come – this month sets the tone for a bright and flourishing year ahead.

MONKEY

The past year has been lively and full of adventure, paving the way for an even more dynamic start. January brings high energy and optimism – success is within reach if you stay focused. Financial prospects are positive, with opportunities for extra income or growth. As you move into the fast-paced Fire Horse year, look after your health and maintain balance. Confidence and preparation will help you soar.

ROOSTER

Reflecting on the past year, you'll find many valuable lessons and accomplishments to be proud of. As the Fire Horse year unfolds, your focus should shift toward refinement and readiness. Use this transitional month to review your goals, refine strategies, and strengthen your foundation. With a positive mindset and clear direction, the months ahead promise recognition, vitality, and renewed success.

DOG

You've weathered the highs and lows of the past year with courage and perseverance. Now, as you step into the bold energy of the Fire Horse year, reflection and recalibration are key. Take time to honour your journey and extract the lessons learned. The coming months bring opportunities for personal growth, meaningful connections, and fresh beginnings. Move forward with faith and optimism – the best is yet to come.

PIG

Though parts of the previous year demanded patience, your steady approach has carried you through successfully. Be proud of how far you've come. The Fire Horse year opens with vibrant, uplifting energy – inspiring creativity, confidence, and renewal. Allow this fresh start to motivate you to expand your horizons, refine your goals, and trust in the flow of abundance that is unfolding.

01 | JANUARY 2026

The Fire Horse Year

---

15 Thursday
Animal: **Earth Ox**
Flying Star: **8**
Good Day: **Rat**
Bad Day: **Goat**

---

16 Friday
Animal: **Metal Tiger**
Flying Star: **9**
Good Day: **Pig**
Bad Day: **Monkey**

---

17 Saturday
Animal: **Metal Rabbit**
Flying Star: **1**
Good Day: **Dog**
Bad Day: **Rooster**

---

18 Sunday
Animal: **Water Dragon**
Flying Star: **2**
Good Day: **Rooster**
Bad Day: **Dog**

---

19 Monday
Animal: **Water Snake**
Flying Star: **3**
Good Day: **Monkey**
Bad Day: **Pig**

---

20 Tuesday
Animal: **Wood Horse**
Flying Star: **4**
Good Day: **Goat**
Bad Day: **Rat**

---

21 Wednesday
Animal: **Wood Goat**
Flying Star: **5**
Good Day: **Horse**
Bad Day: **Ox**

CHINESE ZODIAC ANIMAL RELATIONSHIPS

Understanding the connections between Chinese zodiac animals is a powerful tool that can help you foster stronger everyday interactions. Each animal has a secret friend, allies, and a clashing animal that influences compatibility and connection. By grasping these relationships, you can navigate your personal and professional life with more confidence and insight.

The table below outlines the relationships for each zodiac animal, making it easy to identify your own and note your secret friend, allies, and clashing animals. This practical information provides insights that can guide your ability to form positive connections and navigate interactions with more harmony and understanding.

ANIMAL SIGN	SECRET FRIEND	ALLIES	CLASH ANIMAL
Rat	Ox	Dragon, Monkey	Horse
Ox	Rat	Snake, Rooster	Goat
Tiger	Pig	Horse, Dog	Monkey
Rabbit	Dog	Goat, Pig	Rooster
Dragon	Rooster	Rat, Monkey	Dog
Snake	Monkey	Ox, Rooster	Pig
Horse	Goat	Tiger, Dog	Rat
Goat	Horse	Rabbit, Pig	Ox
Monkey	Snake	Rat, Dragon	Tiger
Rooster	Dragon	Ox, Snake	Rabbit
Dog	Rabbit	Tiger, Horse	Dragon
Pig	Tiger	Rabbit, Goat	Snake

Your secret friend provides protection and symbolises attraction and harmony, while your allies represent ideal matches in relationships and business partnerships.

There is a fundamental principle that an animal prefers to combine rather than clash. This principle, which states that a combination will take priority over a clash, is a critical insight that can guide your understanding of these relationships.

A clash means hindrance, conflict, and disharmony.

Example: If a Horse sees a Rat and a Goat simultaneously, the Goat will combine and be attracted to the Horse and not clash with the Rat. So, you can use this principle to dissolve a clash between two animals.

01 | JANUARY 2026

The Fire Horse Year

22 Thursday
Animal: **Fire Monkey**
Flying Star: **6**
Good Day: **Snake**
Bad Day: **Tiger**

23 Friday
Animal: **Fire Rooster**
Flying Star: **7**
Good Day: **Dragon**
Bad Day: **Rabbit**

24 Saturday
Animal: **Earth Dog**
Flying Star: **8**
Good Day: **Rabbit**
Bad Day: **Dragon**

25 Sunday
Animal: **Earth Pig**
Flying Star: **9**
Good Day: **Tiger**
Bad Day: **Snake**

26 Monday
Animal: **Metal Rat**
Flying Star: **1**
Good Day: **Ox**
Bad Day: **Horse**

27 Tuesday
Animal: **Metal Ox**
Flying Star: **2**
Good Day: **Rat**
Bad Day: **Goat**

28 Wednesday
Animal: **Water Tiger**
Flying Star: **3**
Good Day: **Pig**
Bad Day: **Monkey**

01 | JANUARY 2026

The Fire Horse Year

29 Thursday

Animal: **Water Rabbit**
Flying Star: **4**
Good Day: **Dog**
Bad Day: **Rooster**

30 Friday

Animal: **Wood Dragon**
Flying Star: **5**
Good Day: **Rooster**
Bad Day: **Dog**

31 Saturday

Animal: **Water Snake**
Flying Star: **6**
Good Day: **Monkey**
Bad Day: **Pig**

1 Sunday

Animal: **Fire Horse**
Flying Star: **7**
Good Day: **Goat**
Bad Day: **Rat**

2 Monday

Animal: **Fire Goat**
Flying Star: **8**
Good Day: **Horse**
Bad Day: **Ox**

3 Tuesday

Animal: **Earth Monkey**
Flying Star: **9**
Good Day: **Snake**
Bad Day: **Tiger**

4 Wednesday

Animal: **Earth Rooster**
Flying Star: **1**
Good Day: **Dragon**
Bad Day: **Rabbit**

February 4 – March 5 is the Month of the Tiger

Tiger Chinese Horoscope 2025: Navigating Challenges and Prosperity

Tiger Birth Years: 1926, 1938, 1950, 1962, 1974, 1986, 1998, 2010, 2022, 2034

TIGER – A Year of Confidence, Courage, and Expansion in the Symbolic Cycle

2026 brings a surge of vibrant energy for those born under the bold and adventurous sign of the Tiger. The Yang Fire Horse year ignites your natural confidence, amplifying your charisma and drive to take bold leaps forward. This is a year of movement, recognition, and empowerment, as the Horse and Tiger share a naturally harmonious and mutually supportive relationship in Chinese astrology. Both signs value freedom, courage, and authenticity, and together they create an energetic alignment that fuels success and excitement across every area of life.

You'll feel more motivated, inspired, and courageous than you have in years. The universe seems to open doors just as you arrive, supporting your ambitions and amplifying your leadership. If you've been waiting for the right time to make a daring move – this is it.

Career & Opportunities

The synergy between the Tiger and the Fire Horse favours progress, recognition, and adventure. You'll naturally attract opportunities that align with your passions, creativity, and leadership style. Whether you're in business, management, or creative industries, expect a faster pace and greater visibility.

Your ideas will be well-received, and you may find yourself offered promotions, leadership roles, or expansion opportunities—especially if you're open to travel, relocation, or exploring new territories.

The challenge, however, lies in focus. The Fire Horse energy is fast-moving, and while it lifts your momentum, it can also scatter your attention. Be sure to stay grounded, complete what you start, and avoid jumping too quickly from one vision to another.

Tip: Say yes to bold opportunities—but follow through with discipline and clear strategy.

Wealth & Prosperity

Financially, the outlook for the Tigers in 2026 is strong and promising. The Fire Horse year stimulates growth, career advancement, and profitable ventures, especially for those who are proactive and innovative.

Expect improvements in income, new business ideas, and potential partnerships that enhance financial stability. However, this fiery energy also **brings impulsive tendencies**, particularly around spending or speculative investments.

Your natural enthusiasm may tempt you to act before calculating the risk—so temper excitement with careful planning. Building long-term financial reserves and focusing on steady growth will help you sustain prosperity.

Tip: Enjoy the rewards of success, but channel your fire into financial mastery—save and invest wisely while your momentum is strong.

Love & Relationships

The Fire Horse enhances your magnetism, passion, and confidence—making this an exciting and emotionally fulfilling year. For those in relationships, shared goals, travel, and adventure will deepen bonds and reignite romance. You'll find your connection strengthened through mutual encouragement and honest communication.

Singles are in for a dynamic year of attraction and opportunity. Your natural charisma is amplified, drawing new admirers into your orbit. While many encounters will be fun and passionate, meaningful relationships are also favoured if you stay authentic and grounded.

Family ties are generally warm, though the high energy of the Fire Horse may occasionally spark impatience or frustration. A little diplomacy and humour will smooth any friction.

Tip: Keep your heart open but your expectations balanced. Love thrives this year when shared with laughter, understanding, and mutual respect.

Health & Well-being

Your vitality is high this year, but so is your tendency to burn the candle at both ends. The intensity of the Fire Horse may drive you to overextend yourself, leading to exhaustion if balance isn't maintained.

Pay attention to **your liver, eyes, and cardiovascular system, as stress** and late nights can weaken resilience. Adopt consistent routines for exercise, nutrition, and relaxation. Practices like yoga, meditation, or outdoor movement help ground fiery energy and prevent burnout.

Tip: Channel your fire wisely—build rhythm into your days so your energy remains strong and steady.

Symbolism of the Tiger and Fire Horse

- The Tiger symbolises courage, leadership, and vision—a sign of bold exploration and personal independence.
- The Fire Horse symbolises passion, adventure, and liberation. It represents movement, freedom, and transformation.

Together, they form a dynamic duo of courage and action. The Tiger's strength and strategy, combined with the Horse's fire and enthusiasm, create a year of exhilarating forward movement. This is your time to lead with heart, act with courage, and embody the spirit of fearless authenticity.

Final Overview Tip for 2026

This is your year to take charge and make things happen. The Fire Horse fuels your adventurous spirit and supports your desire for change, growth, and recognition. Lead with integrity, manage your energy, and stay grounded in purpose. When courage meets clarity, success naturally follows – and 2026 is your invitation to shine.

FEBRUARY, Flying Star 8: Unveiling Abundant Prosperity

February ushers in a steady wave of prosperity with the presence of the retiring Flying Star 8. Within the grand celestial orchestra, this star shines brilliantly as the Star of Prosperity, casting an encompassing glow of wealth, well-being, luxury, renown, financial prowess, and lasting success. Flying Star 8 is a beacon of affluence, bringing monetary fortune, nobility, and enduring stability. Under its benevolent light, one can anticipate increased income, financial triumphs, and the fortunate alignment of power and influence. As its radiant energy resonates, professional pursuits flourish, enhancing reputation and recognition for hard work. To align with this favourable tide is to unlock a world of growing potential.

For homes with an East-facing main door or a living or family area in this sector, Flying Star 8's optimistic energy becomes an all-encompassing blessing, especially for the eldest son and those born under the Rabbit sign.

Maintaining a clutter-free space in this sector ensures a smooth energy flow. To activate and amplify its auspicious vibrations, incorporating wealth-related symbols serves as a powerful enhancer. These symbols might include a Buddha figurine, a tassel adorned with 6 Gold Coins, a Wealth God figure, or Gold Ingots. Additionally, strategically placing bright lights, clocks, and televisions, and fostering a bustling environment, significantly boost the star's positive influence. Notably, movement—whether through footsteps or other dynamic actions—remains the most potent conductor of energy in this space.

Flying Star 8's brilliance unveils a realm of luxury and affluence. To embrace its blessings is to enter a world of enduring prosperity and unyielding success.

In 2026, the East sector of the Luo Shu or Bagua School of Feng Shui will be graced by the annual Flying Star 8. This sector, deeply associated with health, longevity, and overall well-being, provides a prime opportunity to enhance these vital aspects of life.

The Wood element governs the East, and incorporating both Wood and Water elements can amplify its positive influence on health and vitality. One practical remedy is to place bamboo in a water feature, as this combination strengthens the Wood element and supports a flourishing state of health. Introducing greenery, plants, and vibrant flowers will further invigorate this sector. The East is also home to the celestial Green Dragon, a symbol of auspicious fortune. Positioning a dragon figurine in this area can optimise the family's luck and overall well-being. Consider placing a Quan Yin statue to safeguard and nurture your physical and emotional vitality, enhancing your protection and health.

Refer to page 12 for this month flying star chart

02 | FEBRUARY 2026

The Fire Horse Year

5 Thursday
Animal: **Metal Dog**
Flying Star: **2**
Good Day: **Rabbit**
Bad Day: **Dragon**

6 Friday
Animal: **Metal Pig**
Flying Star: **3**
Good Day: **Tiger**
Bad Day: **Snake**

7 Saturday
Animal: **Water Rat**
Flying Star: **4**
Good Day: **Ox**
Bad Day: **Horse**

8 Sunday
Animal: **Water Ox**
Flying Star: **5**
Good Day: **Rat**
Bad Day: **Goat**

9 Monday
Animal: **Wood Tiger**
Flying Star: **6**
Good Day: **Pig**
Bad Day: **Monkey**

10 Tuesday
Animal: **Wood Rabbit**
Flying Star: **7**
Good Day: **Dog**
Bad Day: **Rooster**

11 Wednesday
Animal: **Fire Dragon**
Flying Star: **8**
Good Day: **Rooster**
Bad Day: **Dog**

FEBRUARY MONTHLY 2026 CHINESE ZODIAC OVERVIEW

RAT

A lively and fast-paced month sets the tone for new beginnings. You may find yourself juggling several opportunities at once – stay adaptable and grounded to make the most of them. Avoid rushing decisions or letting others dictate your pace. By trusting your instincts and moving with calm precision, you'll turn challenges into stepping stones for growth.

OX

A joyful and auspicious month greets you with optimism and renewed drive. The festive energy inspires confidence, motivation, and connection. Work matters flow smoothly, though your new ideas will benefit from careful structure and planning. Socially, delightful encounters bring inspiration and support. Bask in the vibrant start to the year – this is a time to shine and celebrate life's abundance.

TIGER

The year begins with a burst of vibrant, fast-moving energy. Clarify your goals early and channel your enthusiasm into a clear plan of action. Work and business matters gain traction, and opportunities arise through confident communication. Keep your energy balanced and avoid scattering your focus – a steady pace will help you harness the Fire Horse year's momentum effectively.

RABBIT

The vibrant energy of the Fire Horse year brings joy, inspiration, and fresh opportunities your way. Work and business progress smoothly, yet it's important not to overcommit or promise more than you can deliver. Patience and consistency will be your best allies. Stay centred, manage your energy wisely, and success will naturally follow.

DRAGON

As the vibrant Fire Horse year unfolds, you may feel its fast-paced energy stirring restlessness and pressure. Keep life simple and balanced – good nutrition, rest, and grounding practices are essential. Progress at work may start slowly, so focus on building momentum steadily rather than forcing outcomes. Family dynamics may require patience; gentle communication and understanding will help maintain peace at home.

SNAKE

The vibrant optimism of the Fire Horse year sparks motivation and forward movement. Life picks up speed, calling for quick yet thoughtful decisions. Financial flow is stable, though impulsive spending should be avoided. If considering a job change or new venture, pause to assess carefully – haste could lead to regret. Clarity and patience are your best allies this month.

02 | FEBRUARY
2026

The Fire Horse Year

12
Thursday

Animal: **Fire Snake**
Flying Star: **9**
Good Day: **Monkey**
Bad Day: **Pig**

13
Friday

Animal: **Earth Horse**
Flying Star: **1**
Good Day: **Goat**
Bad Day: **Rat**

✈️ 💇 🎉 💊 🏠

14
Saturday

Animal: **Earth Goat**
Flying Star: **2**
Good Day: **Horse**
Bad Day: **Ox**

🧑‍🌾 🗃️

15
Sunday

Animal: **Metal Monkey**
Flying Star: **3**
Good Day: **Snake**
Bad Day: **Tiger**

16
Monday

Animal: **Metal Rooster**
Flying Star: **4**
Good Day: **Dragon**
Bad Day: **Rabbit**

🗃️ ❤️

17
Tuesday

Animal: **Water Dog**
Flying Star: **5**
Good Day: **Rabbit**
Bad Day: **Dragon**

⚡

18
Wednesday

Animal: **Water Pig**
Flying Star: **6**
Good Day: **Tiger**
Bad Day: **Snake**

🐎

2026 Chinese Astrology Planner

HORSE

Your ruling year begins with a surge of vibrant, fiery momentum. The powerful Yang Fire Horse energy ignites confidence, motivation, and bold vision. You'll feel ready to gallop forward, but balance enthusiasm with patience – not every path requires speed. Focus on your goals, pace your energy, and nurture harmony through mindfulness and self-care. When you ride this wave with grace, outstanding achievements follow.

GOAT

The warm and lively energy of the Fire Horse year inspires motivation and possibility. New beginnings are favoured, though growth will unfold gradually – patience will be your greatest strength. Partnerships and collaborations formed now will be harmonious and supportive. Socially, the month is vibrant, with exciting opportunities for singles to connect and expand their circles.

MONKEY

Energy fluctuates as the year begins, calling for patience and adaptability. Plans may move more slowly than expected, but steady persistence will yield results. Financial stability is present, though impulsive decisions could upset your balance. Relationships benefit from understanding and flexibility – avoid overreacting to minor issues. Prioritise self-care and maintain a positive mindset to keep harmony throughout the month.

ROOSTER

The year begins with confidence and promise, as uplifting energy surrounds the Rooster sign. Supportive influences boost your progress across all areas – career, education, relationships, and finances. This is a powerful month to set intentions and take decisive action toward your goals. With focus and enthusiasm, success will follow naturally.

DOG

The Fire Horse year opens with vibrant and inspiring energy. Excitement fills your path, bringing renewed purpose and drive. Career and finances remain steady, with opportunities for progress and modest gains. Amid the activity, remember to prioritise rest, safety, and self-care. A balanced start now sets the tone for a smooth and successful year ahead.

PIG

The Fire Horse year begins on a wave of optimism and promise. Auspicious influences surround you, enhancing charm, confidence, and motivation. Relationships flourish under this bright energy, and social interactions feel natural and fulfilling. Work brings progress, though a busy schedule may test your stamina. Keep energy balanced through rest, nourishment, and moments of calm reflection.

02 | FEBRUARY 2026

The Fire Horse Year

19 Thursday
Animal: **Wood Rat**
Flying Star: **7**
Good Day: **Ox**
Bad Day: **Horse**

20 Friday
Animal: **Wood Ox**
Flying Star: **8**
Good Day: **Rat**
Bad Day: **Goat**

21 Saturday
Animal: **Fire Tiger**
Flying Star: **9**
Good Day: **Pig**
Bad Day: **Monkey**

22 Sunday
Animal: **Fire Rabbit**
Flying Star: **1**
Good Day: **Dog**
Bad Day: **Rooster**

23 Monday
Animal: **Earth Dragon**
Flying Star: **2**
Good Day: **Rooster**
Bad Day: **Dog**

24 Tuesday
Animal: **Earth Snake**
Flying Star: **3**
Good Day: **Monkey**
Bad Day: **Pig**

25 Wednesday
Animal: **Metal Horse**
Flying Star: **4**
Good Day: **Goat**
Bad Day: **Rat**

02 | FEBRUARY 2026

The Fire Horse Year

26 Thursday
Animal: **Metal Goat**
Flying Star: **5**
Good Day: **Horse**
Bad Day: **Ox**

27 Friday
Animal: **Water Monkey**
Flying Star: **6**
Good Day: **Snake**
Bad Day: **Tiger**

28 Saturday
Animal: **Water Rooster**
Flying Star: **7**
Good Day: **Dragon**
Bad Day: **Rabbit**

1 Sunday
Animal: **Wood Dog**
Flying Star: **8**
Good Day: **Rabbit**
Bad Day: **Dragon**

2 Monday
Animal: **Wood Pig**
Flying Star: **9**
Good Day: **Tiger**
Bad Day: **Snake**

3 Tuesday
Animal: **Fire Rat**
Flying Star: **1**
Good Day: **Ox**
Bad Day: **Horse**

4 Wednesday
Animal: **Fire Ox**
Flying Star: **2**
Good Day: **Rat**
Bad Day: **Goat**

March 6 – April 4 is the Month of the Rabbit

Rabbit Chinese Horoscope 2025: Navigating Challenges and Embracing Opportunities

Rabbit Birth Years: 1915, 1927, 1939, 1951, 1963, 1975, 1987, 1999, 2011, 2023, 2035

RABBIT – A Year of Joy, Expansion, and Renewed Optimism in the Fire Horse Cycle

2026 unfolds as a bright and buoyant year for those born under the graceful and intuitive sign of the Rabbit. The Yang Fire Horse brings excitement, vitality, and opportunity – encouraging you to step out of your comfort zone and embrace life with optimism and enthusiasm. While your natural rhythm prefers calm and harmony, the Fire Horse invites you to be bolder, more expressive, and open to adventure.

Fortunately, you're supported by a cluster of auspicious stars surrounding the Rabbit this year. These celestial influences enhance your luck, charisma, and emotional resilience, helping you navigate challenges with grace and magnetism. Even when temporary fluctuations arise, the presence of these positive stars ensures that problems are resolved swiftly, leaving you stronger and wiser.

Career & Opportunities

This is a year of movement and potential professional reshaping. You may experience career transitions, new management, or changes in company structure. While these may initially unsettle your peace-loving nature, they are stepping stones to greater growth and freedom. The Fire Horse favours those who can adapt quickly and think creatively, so lean into change rather than resisting it.

If you've been considering a career shift or entrepreneurial venture, opportunities will appear – but proceed with careful planning. Analyse financial implications and ensure new directions align with your long-term vision. Collaboration and networking are key themes this year, and partnerships with dynamic or creative individuals will bring rewarding progress.

Tip: Trust your instincts, but pair intuition with practicality. Adaptation and diplomacy will keep your professional life flourishing under the Fire Horse's lively pace.

Wealth & Prosperity

Financially, 2026 brings improvement and opportunity, though it also requires mindfulness. The presence of auspicious stars points toward profitable gains, steady income, and positive momentum for most Rabbits. However, the fast-moving Fire Horse may tempt you into impulsive spending or financial overcommitment.

There could be sudden expenses related to family, travel, or business ventures – so ensure you budget carefully and maintain a financial buffer. If you invest, do so with clear intention and reliable advice.

Tip: Prosperity flows when calm meets courage. Manage your finances with clarity, and resist emotional spending triggered by restlessness or excitement.

Love & Relationships

The Fire Horse brings warmth, magnetism, and romantic sparkle to your social world. For Rabbits, this is one of the most socially engaging and love-filled years in recent cycles.

If you are single, new and meaningful connections are highly likely, often emerging through travel, social gatherings, or shared interests. The year's energy enhances your charm, making you especially attractive and approachable.

For those already in relationships, passion, understanding, and communication deepen bonds. Family relationships also blossom under this influence, with increased joy and harmony at home. Even minor disagreements can be easily resolved with warmth and humour.

Tip: Keep your heart open, but your emotions balanced. This is a year to love wholeheartedly, yet wisely.

Health & Well-being

With the energetic Fire Horse stirring activity, you may find yourself busier and more socially engaged than usual. While this brings joy, it also increases the need for rest, grounding, and self-care. Rabbits may be prone to fatigue, digestive discomfort, or restless sleep if they ignore the body's natural rhythm.

To maintain vitality, schedule downtime, eat nourishing foods, and practice calming rituals like meditation, nature walks, or gentle yoga. Remember: rest is not laziness – it's restoration.

Tip: Pace yourself. Balance lively activity with mindful pauses to keep both body and spirit radiant throughout the year.

Symbolism of the Rabbit and Fire Horse

- The Rabbit symbolises grace, diplomacy, and intuitive intelligence. It represents peace, refinement, and the ability to create beauty and harmony even amid change.
- The Fire Horse symbolises adventure, passion, and motion – it sparks courage and creativity, encouraging bold moves and personal reinvention.

Together, these energies blend grace with courage – the Rabbit's gentleness softens the Horse's fire, while the Horse's dynamism ignites the Rabbit's spirit. This creates a year of balanced growth, joyful evolution, and renewed vitality.

Final Overview Tip for 2026

This is your year to shine with confidence and charm. Embrace the Fire Horse's enthusiasm but stay grounded in your inner peace. Opportunities will abound when you trust your intuition, maintain emotional balance, and follow joy. Keep your heart light, your mind open, and your energy balanced – and the year will reward you with happiness, harmony, and abundance.

MARCH, Flying Star 7: A Multitude of Discord and Unrest

March heralds a period of unrest with the arrival of the ominous Flying Star 7. In the intricate cosmic dance, this inauspicious star ushers in a cacophony of conflict, disputes, legal entanglements, ailments, mishaps, theft, and the unsettling echoes of gossip. The shadow cast by Flying Star 7 is profoundly feared, as it has the potential to sow seeds of rivalry, trespass, theft, and even violence into the fabric of life. During this phase, caution is essential, as one must navigate its treacherous currents with care.

The unsettling energies of this star are particularly potent in matters of emotional and physical well-being, making vigilance crucial for the matriarchs, mothers, older women, or those born under the Goat or Monkey zodiac sign. In professional environments, office politics swell, and rivalries intensify. Trust must be earned as deception and schemes lurk beneath the surface. The Southwest sector, in particular, resonates with this turbulence, and therefore, heightened awareness and vigilance are vital to maintaining tranquillity.

Flying Star 7 also increases the risk of mouth and tooth ailments, potentially requiring hospitalisation or surgical interventions for those with pre-existing health issues. Traditional remedies become essential in mitigating its disruptive influence. One such remedy involves placing three pieces of bamboo in a clear glass vase filled with water in the Western sector. The symbolic talisman of the Evil Eye, flanked by seven glass elephants, serves as a powerful countermeasure. Positioning a Blue Rhinoceros and a Blue Elephant can protect against this evil energy. As a final safeguard, incorporating a water feature helps to neutralise the metallic energy dominating this space, ensuring the tranquillity and vitality of the surrounding environment.

Flying Star 7's arrival necessitates a mindful approach, as its discordant energies require careful navigation to avoid being swept into its currents of unrest and discord.

In 2026, the Southwest sector of the Luo Shu or Bagua School of Feng Shui will host the annual Flying Star 7. This sector is pivotal for fostering relationship luck, love, romance, and marriage, making it a vital area for enhancing these aspects of life.

The Southwest is associated with the Earth element, and to amplify its positive effects on relationships, integrating both Earth and Fire energies is critical. Enhance this sector with amethyst or rose quartz crystals, and consider incorporating vibrant hues such as purple, pink, and red peonies to support romantic endeavours. The double happiness symbol and a pair of Mandarin Ducks are traditional symbols that signify love and partnership, making them ideal for this area. To further boost the energy, add bright lighting to the Southwest sector to illuminate it with positive, nurturing vibrations.

Refer to page 12 for this month flying star chart

03 | MARCH 2026

The Fire Horse Year

5 Thursday
Animal: **Earth Tiger**
Flying Star: **3**
Good Day: **Pig**
Bad Day: **Monkey**

6 Friday
Animal: **Earth Rabbit**
Flying Star: **4**
Good Day: **Dog**
Bad Day: **Rooster**

7 Saturday
Animal: **Metal Dragon**
Flying Star: **5**
Good Day: **Rooster**
Bad Day: **Dog**

8 Sunday
Animal: **Metal Snake**
Flying Star: **6**
Good Day: **Monkey**
Bad Day: **Pig**

9 Monday
Animal: **Water Horse**
Flying Star: **7**
Good Day: **Goat**
Bad Day: **Rat**

10 Tuesday
Animal: **Water Goat**
Flying Star: **8**
Good Day: **Horse**
Bad Day: **Ox**

11 Wednesday
Animal: **Wood Monkey**
Flying Star: **9**
Good Day: **Snake**
Bad Day: **Tiger**

MARCH MONTHLY 2026 CHINESE ZODIAC OVERVIEW

RAT

This month's energy may stir self-doubt or emotional restlessness. Focus on clarity, not confusion. When uncertainty arises, pause, breathe, and realign with your purpose. Confidence is your best ally – commit to your goals and trust the process. Balance your drive with moments of rest to prevent burnout.

OX

The month's energy feels demanding, and emotions may run high. Avoid confrontations or impulsive reactions. Patience and tact will protect your relationships and peace of mind. Financially, it's best to adopt moderation – spend wisely and avoid unnecessary risks. Loved ones may require extra understanding, so practice compassion and calm communication.

TIGER

A slower rhythm settles in, inviting you to review finances and strengthen your foundations. Supportive and influential individuals may appear, offering guidance or collaboration. Take a cautious approach to investments or new ventures – avoid impulsive decisions and ensure all details are well-researched. Stability now sets the stage for lasting growth.

RABBIT

Momentum continues with a bright and confident flow. Work and business matters reach a rewarding peak, and your efforts begin to bear visible results. Make the most of the first half of the month, as things may slow slightly later. Guard against envy from others and protect your accomplishments with grace and discretion.

DRAGON

Supportive yet slightly demanding energy surrounds this month. Minor hurdles may surface at work or in business, but staying calm and flexible will help you navigate them with ease. Clear communication and careful decision-making are key. Both personal and professional areas benefit from steady, thoughtful effort rather than haste.

SNAKE

A productive and supportive energy surrounds you, bringing strength to both work and business. Collaborations flow smoothly, and progress can be made with ease. Maintain diplomacy to avoid unnecessary conflict. Relationships, both personal and familial, enjoy peace and understanding. Financial stability continues, bringing a calm and balanced month overall.

03 | MARCH 2026

The Fire Horse Year

12 Thursday
Animal: **Wood Rooster**
Flying Star: **1**
Good Day: **Dragon**
Bad Day: **Rabbit**

13 Friday
Animal: **Fire Dog**
Flying Star: **2**
Good Day: **Rabbit**
Bad Day: **Dragon**

✈️ 🔪 🎰 🗳️ 🎉 🏠

14 Saturday
Animal: **Fire Pig**
Flying Star: **3**
Good Day: **Tiger**
Bad Day: **Snake**

🗳️ 🎉 🔪 🏠

15 Sunday
Animal: **Earth Rat**
Flying Star: **4**
Good Day: **Ox**
Bad Day: **Horse**

💇 ❤️

16 Monday
Animal: **Earth Ox**
Flying Star: **5**
Good Day: **Rat**
Bad Day: **Goat**

⚡ 🏠

17 Tuesday
Animal: **Metal Tiger**
Flying Star: **6**
Good Day: **Pig**
Bad Day: **Monkey**

🗳️ 🔪

18 Wednesday
Animal: **Metal Rabbit**
Flying Star: **7**
Good Day: **Dog**
Bad Day: **Rooster**

🎉 ✈️

HORSE

Dynamic energy continues to flow, bringing opportunities for growth and success. Consistency is key – stay disciplined and complete what you start. In business, strengthening professional relationships will open new doors. Socially, joy and connection abound. Singles are especially favoured this month, with romance likely to emerge naturally through shared interests and lively gatherings.

GOAT

Change is in the air. Shifts in your environment or career may arise, encouraging flexibility and open-mindedness. Avoid forcing outcomes—let events unfold naturally. If you're considering a new career path, this is a favourable month to explore options. Financial energy remains steady, but mindful spending will help maintain balance.

MONKEY

The pace quickens, and optimism returns. Work and career matters progress smoothly when approached with clarity and organisation. This is an excellent time to reconnect socially or expand your circle. Singles may meet new and inspiring people. Financial energy remains steady, though significant investments should still be made cautiously. Spend time outdoors or enjoy short breaks to restore vitality.

ROOSTER

The energy this month is more delicate, calling for emotional awareness and diplomacy. Changes in your work environment may arise, but how you communicate and respond will determine the outcome. Keep conversations clear and constructive to prevent misunderstandings. Balance and calm action will help you navigate smoothly.

DOG

Energy slows this month, encouraging patience as projects or plans unfold more gradually. Delays may test your tolerance, but perseverance will pay off. Keep communication clear and flexible at work – diplomacy will prevent misunderstandings. On a positive note, this is a favourable time for travel, exploration, and expanding your horizons.

PIG

Momentum continues, bringing inspiration and fertile ground for fresh ideas. This is an excellent month for planning, learning, or developing new business or academic goals. Supportive people and opportunities will appear once you're ready to take action. With energy levels high, remember to pace yourself – maintain balance between productivity and self-care to keep vitality strong.

03 | MARCH
2026

The Fire Horse Year

19 Thursday
- Animal: **Water Dragon**
- Flying Star: **8**
- Good Day: **Rooster**
- Bad Day: **Dog**

20 Friday
- Animal: **Water Snake**
- Flying Star: **9**
- Good Day: **Monkey**
- Bad Day: **Pig**

🎉 ✒️

21 Saturday
- Animal: **Wood Horse**
- Flying Star: **1**
- Good Day: **Goat**
- Bad Day: **Rat**

22 Sunday
- Animal: **Wood Goat**
- Flying Star: **2**
- Good Day: **Horse**
- Bad Day: **Ox**

💼 ✈️ 🏠

23 Monday
- Animal: **Fire Monkey**
- Flying Star: **3**
- Good Day: **Snake**
- Bad Day: **Tiger**

🗳️ ✈️ 🏠

24 Tuesday
- Animal: **Fire Rooster**
- Flying Star: **4**
- Good Day: **Dragon**
- Bad Day: **Rabbit**

❤️

25 Wednesday
- Animal: **Earth Dog**
- Flying Star: **5**
- Good Day: **Rabbit**
- Bad Day: **Dragon**

⚡ 💿 ✒️

03 | MARCH 2026

The Fire Horse Year

26 Thursday
Animal: **Earth Pig**
Flying Star: **6**
Good Day: **Tiger**
Bad Day: **Snake**

27 Friday
Animal: **Metal Rat**
Flying Star: **7**
Good Day: **Ox**
Bad Day: **Horse**

28 Saturday
Animal: **Metal Ox**
Flying Star: **8**
Good Day: **Rat**
Bad Day: **Goat**

29 Sunday
Animal: **Water Tiger**
Flying Star: **9**
Good Day: **Pig**
Bad Day: **Monkey**

30 Monday
Animal: **Water Rabbit**
Flying Star: **1**
Good Day: **Dog**
Bad Day: **Rooster**

31 Tuesday
Animal: **Wood Dragon**
Flying Star: **2**
Good Day: **Rooster**
Bad Day: **Dog**

1 Wednesday
Animal: **Wood Snake**
Flying Star: **3**
Good Day: **Monkey**
Bad Day: **Pig**

2026 Chinese Astrology Planner

April 5 – May 5 is the Month of the Dragon

Dragon Chinese Horoscope 2025: The Year of Transformation and Passion

Dragon Birth Years: 1916, 1928, 1940, 1952, 1964, 1976, 1988, 2000, 2012, 2024, 2036

DRAGON – A Year of Strategy, Balance, and Quiet Power in the Fire Horse Cycle

In 2026, the Yang Fire Horse year invites the magnificent Dragon to navigate a cycle of both challenge and opportunity – a year that tests your wisdom, adaptability, and emotional mastery. While the Fire Horse brings momentum, transformation, and movement, specific astrological influences may also trigger moments of restlessness or inner tension. Yet, as one of the most regal and resilient signs, you possess all the insight and charisma needed to turn challenges into triumphs.

This is a year that rewards patience, gentleness, and balance. By leading with flexibility rather than force, and by staying grounded amidst rapid change, you'll find that progress continues steadily – even when the winds of uncertainty blow.

Career & Opportunities

Professionally, the year ahead calls for mindful navigation. The Fire Horse injects dynamic, high-paced energy into your work life, bringing both opportunity and added pressure. You may face heavier workloads, tight deadlines, or shifting priorities that demand quick thinking and emotional composure.

Stay organised, delegate wisely, and focus on strategic time management – this will be the key to your success. New projects may arise, and while they hold great promise, resist the urge to overextend yourself. When you balance action with reflection, your leadership will shine.

The good news is that career advancement and recognition are entirely possible this year, particularly if you demonstrate diplomacy and calm under pressure. Promotions or new collaborations may arise through adaptability and the maintenance of strong professional alliances.

Tip: Embrace change as an ally. The Fire Horse rewards those who adjust their stride while keeping their eye on the long game.

Wealth & Prosperity

Financially, the Dragon's outlook for 2026 is steady, with potential for gradual growth through discipline and prudence. Your income remains stable, and financial rewards will align directly with your level of effort and consistency.

However, this is not a year for risk-taking or speculative ventures. The fiery pace of the Horse can tempt you into impulsive decisions or grand financial gestures – but restraint and careful planning will safeguard your prosperity. Avoid unnecessary loans, overspending, or investments made under pressure.

Instead, focus on budgeting, consolidating resources, and long-term planning. If you stay steady and thoughtful, the financial seeds you plant this year will mature beautifully in the years to come.

Tip: Prosperity favours patience. Let wisdom, not impulse, guide your hand in money matters.

Love & Relationships

The Fire Horse's fast-moving energy can create ripples in your emotional world, particularly if work demands consume too much of your time. The Dragon's natural ambition may unintentionally sideline personal connections, so maintaining emotional presence and balance becomes essential.

For those in relationships, this is a year to nurture connection through attention and appreciation. Spend quality time with loved ones, listen with compassion, and share your thoughts openly. When you express both vulnerability and strength, bonds deepen beautifully.

Singles may encounter interesting romantic possibilities through travel, career circles, or new social settings. However, patience is again your ally – the most meaningful relationships will unfold gradually and authentically.

Tip: Love thrives when time and attention are given freely—Prioritise heart connection alongside ambition.

Health & Well-being

With a demanding year ahead, your physical and emotional balance are top priorities. The Fire Horse's pace may overstimulate your system, leading to fatigue if rest is ignored. Integrate regular breaks, nourishing food, and calming practices into your routine.

Travel is strongly indicated this year and will be both refreshing and healing – a change of scenery will restore your energy and provide new inspiration. Gentle exercise, such as swimming, tai chi, or yoga, will help balance Fire energy and calm the mind.

Tip: Move often, rest deeply, and protect your inner peace as you would your greatest treasure.

Symbolism of the Dragon and Fire Horse

- The Dragon symbolises wisdom, power, and transformation. It is the visionary of the zodiac – ambitious, creative, and driven by noble ideals.
- The Fire Horse embodies passion, motion, and courage – it inspires bold action, adventure, and reinvention.

Together, this combination forms a potent blend of vision and vitality. The Dragon's intellect and leadership harmonise with the Horse's fiery enthusiasm, producing a year of transformation – provided that wisdom tempers impulse.

Final Overview Tip for 2026

This is your year to lead with grace, to temper passion with patience, and to balance your grand ambitions with emotional awareness. The Fire Horse amplifies your drive, but it also asks you to slow down when needed and stay mindful of your limits. When wisdom meets action, and heart leads alongside ambition, you will not only succeed – you'll soar.

APRIL 2027, Flying Star 6: A Radiant Beacon of Authority and Fortune

April ushers in the illustrious Flying Star 6, a celestial force that brings the energies of authority, power, wealth, and heavenly luck. This star is a harbinger of prosperous times, orchestrating a grand symphony of career opportunities and the realisation of long-held ambitions. Under its glowing influence, one can expect an infusion of enhanced power, elevated status, and the radiant aura of a commendable reputation. As an emissary of prosperity, Flying Star 6 bestows divine favour upon its beneficiaries, particularly those seeking career advancement and success. Middle-aged men, middle sons, and those born under the Horse zodiac sign are especially poised to reap the rewards of this star's benevolent influence.

The veneration of Flying Star 6's positive attributes can establish a commanding presence, symbolising elevated status and influential sway within professional and social circles. Its energetic current encapsulates the essence of authority, empowering individuals to step into leadership roles and distinction.

To fully awaken the potential of Flying Star 6, one must infuse it with vibrant Yang energy. This can be achieved through the harmonious interplay of water features, resonant sounds, and lively activities. Traditional enhancers, steeped in symbolism, can amplify this star's auspicious energies—whether through the dignified presence of a Horse figurine, the subtle charm of Six Gold Coins suspended from a tassel, or the enduring symbol of Gold Ingots.

However, despite its brilliance, caution is advised. External negative influences can unexpectedly cast shadows over Flying Star 6, turning its blessings into turbulent challenges. Such disruptions may manifest as sudden upheavals, abrupt changes, or even kidney or leg complications.

As Flying Star 6 radiates its potent energies in April, embracing its power with wisdom and awareness can lead to prosperity, authority, and enduring success.

In 2026, the North sector of the Luo Shu or Bagua School of Feng Shui will be graced by the annual Flying Star 6, a key influence on career and business fortune.

The Water element governs the North, and to bolster this sector for optimal career and business success, it is essential to harmonise the Water energy with Metal elements. Enhance the North with metallic colours such as white, silver, gold, pewter, bronze, and black tones to support and balance the Water energy. Incorporate metal décor objects with blue-black accents, and consider adding water-themed pictures or decorative elements to amplify the positive influence. Additionally, placing a Black Tortoise or Dragon Tortoise in this area can further strengthen career prospects and business growth.

Refer to page 12 for this month flying star chart

04 | APRIL 2026

The Fire Horse Year

2 Thursday
Animal: **Fire Horse**
Flying Star: **4**
Good Day: **Goat**
Bad Day: **Rat**
🕯️ ❤️

3 Friday
Animal: **Fire Goat**
Flying Star: **5**
Good Day: **Horse**
Bad Day: **Ox**
⚡ 🗳️ 🕯️ 🎉 💊 🏠

4 Saturday
Animal: **Earth Monkey**
Flying Star: **6**
Good Day: **Snake**
Bad Day: **Tiger**
🗳️ ✈️ 🏠

5 Sunday
Animal: **Earth Rooster**
Flying Star: **7**
Good Day: **Dragon**
Bad Day: **Rabbit**

6 Monday
Animal: **Metal Dog**
Flying Star: **8**
Good Day: **Rabbit**
Bad Day: **Dragon**

7 Tuesday
Animal: **Metal Pig**
Flying Star: **9**
Good Day: **Tiger**
Bad Day: **Snake**

8 Wednesday
Animal: **Water Rat**
Flying Star: **1**
Good Day: **Ox**
Bad Day: **Horse**
🗳️ 💊

APRIL MONTHLY 2026 CHINESE ZODIAC OVERVIEW

RAT

Momentum builds in your professional and financial world. Your efforts are beginning to gain traction, and cooperation with others is bringing tangible progress. If politics or tension surfaces in the workplace, maintain diplomacy – your charm and strategic thinking will win support–a favourable month for career advancement or exploring new roles.

OX

An intense yet slow-moving energy surrounds you, testing your patience and adaptability. Progress at work may feel delayed, but persistence pays off. Keep yourself balanced through physical activity or creative pursuits that calm the mind. Shift your perspective when challenges arise – flexibility will turn obstacles into stepping stones.

TIGER

A surge of positive energy reawakens your motivation. You'll feel inspired to act on ideas that have been in motion since earlier in the year. Harmony in relationships will come through patience and openness – listen as much as you speak. Networking and new social connections prove especially beneficial, paving the way for fruitful alliances.

RABBIT

A slower, more introspective rhythm encourages rest and rebalancing. While this is a good time to recharge, don't lose sight of deadlines or important commitments. Money flow may slow temporarily, so keep spending practically. Use this period to refine your strategies and ensure your next steps are well-planned.

DRAGON

This is a month of unpredictability, where trying to control every detail could invite tension. Flow with change instead of resisting it. Prioritise rest and stress management – the buildup from recent months may surface now, demanding self-care. Relationships may experience temporary strain due to timing delays; patience and honest dialogue will restore harmony. Avoid unnecessary spending and speculative risks.

SNAKE

Strong, fast-moving energy may bring stress or fatigue. Unexpected shifts at work or in plans require flexibility and vigilance. Keep your pace steady – don't burn out trying to control what's beyond reach: Prioritise rest, self-care, and quiet moments to restore balance. A brief getaway or time in nature will be particularly healing.

04 | APRIL 2026

The Fire Horse Year

9 Thursday
Animal: **Water Ox**
Flying Star: **2**
Good Day: **Rat**
Bad Day: **Goat**

10 Friday
Animal: **Wood Tiger**
Flying Star: **3**
Good Day: **Pig**
Bad Day: **Monkey**

11 Saturday
Animal: **Wood Rabbit**
Flying Star: **4**
Good Day: **Dog**
Bad Day: **Rooster**

12 Sunday
Animal: **Fire Dragon**
Flying Star: **5**
Good Day: **Rooster**
Bad Day: **Dog**

13 Monday
Animal: **Fire Snake**
Flying Star: **6**
Good Day: **Monkey**
Bad Day: **Pig**

14 Tuesday
Animal: **Earth Horse**
Flying Star: **7**
Good Day: **Goat**
Bad Day: **Rat**

15 Wednesday
Animal: **Earth Goat**
Flying Star: **8**
Good Day: **Horse**
Bad Day: **Ox**

HORSE

A busy, expansive month unfolds as both work and social obligations increase. Projects nurtured earlier in the year begin to show visible results. Though success is on the horizon, remain attentive to details and practice patience with loved ones. Emotional sensitivity may surface — a calm and understanding approach will keep relationships harmonious.

GOAT

Energy dips slightly, creating feelings of restlessness or uncertainty. Workplace transitions, such as departmental adjustments or new team dynamics, may test your patience. Stay adaptable and avoid conflict, especially with authority figures. In relationships, emotions may run high; gentle communication and empathy will help smooth rough edges.

MONKEY

Energy feels somewhat uneven, and minor work obstacles or delays may appear. Patience and flexibility will ensure smoother outcomes. Short trips or personal development activities — such as workshops or creative pursuits — bring joy and inspiration. In relationships, open and honest communication helps strengthen trust and emotional balance.

ROOSTER

Momentum builds, and progress becomes visible. Work and business matters flow well, and your confidence returns in full force. It's the perfect time to act boldly, expand your ideas, and implement long-term plans. Financial energy is steady, with gains indicated. A lively social calendar brings laughter, joy, and valuable new connections.

DOG

Fast-moving energy takes over, introducing both opportunity and restlessness. Those in roles involving movement, travel, or negotiation will thrive, as luck supports your efforts. Keep all dealings transparent and straightforward to ensure smooth progress. To maintain balance, schedule time for relaxation and avoid overextending yourself.

PIG

A softer rhythm may bring minor obstacles or slowdowns. Don't resist these pauses; they allow you to refine plans and build stronger connections. Patience and adaptability will help you navigate small challenges smoothly. For younger Pigs, cultivating emotional intelligence at work is key. Elders should pay attention to heart and circulation health through a mindful diet and gentle activity.

04 | APRIL 2026

The Fire Horse Year

16 Thursday
Animal: **Metal Monkey**
Flying Star: **9**
Good Day: **Snake**
Bad Day: **Tiger**

17 Friday
Animal: **Metal Rooster**
Flying Star: **1**
Good Day: **Dragon**
Bad Day: **Rabbit**

18 Saturday
Animal: **Water Dog**
Flying Star: **2**
Good Day: **Rabbit**
Bad Day: **Dragon**

19 Sunday
Animal: **Water Pig**
Flying Star: **3**
Good Day: **Tiger**
Bad Day: **Snake**

20 Monday
Animal: **Wood Rat**
Flying Star: **4**
Good Day: **Ox**
Bad Day: **Horse**

21 Tuesday
Animal: **Wood Ox**
Flying Star: **5**
Good Day: **Rat**
Bad Day: **Goat**

22 Wednesday
Animal: **Fire Tiger**
Flying Star: **6**
Good Day: **Pig**
Bad Day: **Monkey**

THE FENG SHUI OF YOUR FRONT DOOR

In 2026, your front door becomes even more critical than usual.

With the Yang Fire Horse galloping through the year, the pace of life speeds up, opportunities move quickly, and the qi entering your home needs to be clean, clear, and well-directed. Your main entrance is the *mouth of qi*—the point where fresh, vibrant energy enters your space and nourishes everyone who lives inside. When the front door is supported, your home feels alive, prosperous, and protected. When it isn't, the Fire Horse's fast energy can easily become scattered, draining, or overwhelming.

As you move into 2026, take time to assess your entrance and make sure it welcomes good fortune—and keeps disruptive energy out.

Watch for "poison arrows" pointing toward your entrance.

Harsh angles, sharp edges, corners of buildings, or aggressive rooflines aimed at the door weaken the qi before it reaches your home. Redirect, shield, or—if the layout allows—relocate the door to a calmer, safer position.

Avoid having the main door directly below a bathroom.

This compresses and weakens the entering qi, which is especially problematic in a Fire Horse year when stability is vital. If possible, shift the entrance along the façade to a more supportive location.

Make sure your front door is not facing a narrow alley or a tight gap between buildings.

In 2026, this kind of "squeezed qi" can trigger health vulnerabilities, financial strain, or emotional tension. If the alignment cannot be changed, strengthen the area with lighting and clear space.

Keep the entrance clear, clean, and uncluttered.

Shoes piled at the doorway, dead plants, or obstacles create stagnant energy. Allow qi to glide in easily—this is essential in a year of rapid movement and opportunity.

Create breathing room in front of the door.

A small open space, bright lighting, or a clear foyer encourages qi to settle gently before flowing inward. This helps attract supportive opportunities and good luck, significant as the Fire Horse amplifies momentum.

Ensure your door is the right size for your home.

A door that's too large can scatter wealth in a year where money moves quickly.

A door that's too small can restrict growth and harmony.

Aim for proportion, balance, and a sense that the entrance feels "right" for the home's scale.

In the Fire Horse year, your front door is far more than an entry point—it is the energetic gateway that determines how you experience speed, progress, and abundance in 2026. When the door is supported, protected, and energetically nourished, the entire home—and everyone within it—thrives.

04 | APRIL 2026

The Fire Horse Year

23 Thursday
Animal: **Fire Rabbit**
Flying Star: **7**
Good Day: **Dog**
Bad Day: **Rooster**

24 Friday
Animal: **Earth Dragon**
Flying Star: **8**
Good Day: **Rooster**
Bad Day: **Dog**

25 Saturday
Animal: **Earth Snake**
Flying Star: **9**
Good Day: **Monkey**
Bad Day: **Pig**

26 Sunday
Animal: **Metal Horse**
Flying Star: **1**
Good Day: **Goat**
Bad Day: **Rat**

27 Monday
Animal: **Metal Goat**
Flying Star: **2**
Good Day: **Horse**
Bad Day: **Ox**

28 Tuesday
Animal: **Water Monkey**
Flying Star: **3**
Good Day: **Snake**
Bad Day: **Tiger**

29 Wednesday
Animal: **Water Rooster**
Flying Star: **4**
Good Day: **Dragon**
Bad Day: **Rabbit**

04 | APRIL 2026

The Fire Horse Year

30 Thursday
Animal: **Wood Dog**
Flying Star: **5**
Good Day: **Rabbit**
Bad Day: **Dragon**

1 Friday
Animal: **Wood Pig**
Flying Star: **6**
Good Day: **Tiger**
Bad Day: **Snake**

2 Saturday
Animal: **Fire Rat**
Flying Star: **7**
Good Day: **Ox**
Bad Day: **Horse**

3 Sunday
Animal: **Fire Ox**
Flying Star: **8**
Good Day: **Rat**
Bad Day: **Goat**

4 Monday
Animal: **Earth Tiger**
Flying Star: **9**
Good Day: **Pig**
Bad Day: **Monkey**

5 Tuesday
Animal: **Earth Rabbit**
Flying Star: **1**
Good Day: **Dog**
Bad Day: **Rooster**

6 Wednesday
Animal: **Metal Dragon**
Flying Star: **2**
Good Day: **Rooster**
Bad Day: **Dog**

May 6 – June 5 is the Month of the Snake

Snake Chinese Horoscope 2025: Navigating Passion and Transformation

Snake Birth Years: 1917, 1929, 1941, 1953, 1965, 1977, 1989, 2001, 2013, 2025, 2037

SNAKE – A Year of Insight, Harmony, and Transformative Growth in the Fire Horse Cycle

In 2026, the Yang Fire Horse brings a year of movement, opportunity, and illumination – and for the wise and intuitive Snake, this energy aligns in a generally harmonious way. The Snake and Horse share a complementary relationship, one built on mutual respect for intelligence, adaptability, and forward motion. This means that, overall, you can look forward to a year that supports progress, confidence, and personal evolution.

However, harmony doesn't always mean smooth sailing. The fiery nature of the Horse can sometimes spark impatience, emotional intensity, or conflict if not balanced. The key for the Snake this year lies in emotional mastery – using your intuition, calm observation, and gentle communication to maintain peace and progress even when the pace feels demanding.

Career & Opportunities

The Fire Horse year encourages movement, reinvention, and enthusiasm in your professional life. For the Snake, this is a time when creativity and intuition combine beautifully with ambition. If you've been contemplating a career shift, exploring a new project, or stepping into leadership, 2026 brings multiple openings – but you'll need to be proactive and alert to seize them.

Your greatest advantage lies in your ability to read between the lines, to sense the undercurrents of situations, and to act strategically. Use this talent wisely, and you'll find yourself recognized and rewarded for your insight and innovation. Those who bring passion and inspiration into their work will stand out and experience genuine success.

Tip: Move with purpose and stay attuned to timing. Act decisively when opportunities align, but avoid pushing against resistance – your intuition will tell you when to strike.

Wealth & Prosperity

Financially, the year offers steady progress and modest gains. Income remains stable, and those with long-term investments or property may experience healthy growth. The Fire Horse energy can amplify enthusiasm for business or investment ventures, but moderation is essential. Avoid impulsive decisions, especially in speculative markets or high-risk deals.

For Snakes who manage finances carefully, 2026 can become a year of quiet accumulation and strategic advancement. If you channel energy into creative or knowledge-based pursuits, the rewards could exceed expectations.

Tip: Prosperity grows through discernment. Focus on sustainability rather than speed – build wealth through wisdom, not impulse.

Love & Relationships

Relationships for the Snake in 2026 are generally positive but require mindfulness. The strong Fire element may heighten emotions, impatience, or restlessness, which can lead to misunderstandings if communication is reactive. Practice tolerance and empathy, especially with loved ones. Small irritations can be quickly resolved when approached with kindness and humor.

For singles, the Fire Horse brings a lively, social year filled with new faces and romantic possibilities. Your natural charm and mysterious aura are magnetic – however, it's wise to remain discerning about who you let into your inner circle.

Those in committed relationships can deepen emotional bonds through shared adventures, honest dialogue, and renewed affection.

Tip: Communication is your compass. Speak gently, listen deeply, and love will flourish.

Health & Well-being

The Snake is sensitive to energetic fluctuations, and with the fiery Horse ruling the year, stress management becomes essential. The Fire element governs the heart, blood, and circulation – areas to watch carefully. In addition, digestive and kidney health may need extra attention, particularly if lifestyle habits have become indulgent or inconsistent.

To maintain balance, practice moderation in food, alcohol, and work hours. Gentle exercise like tai chi,such as meditation, qigong, or gentle yoga – willharmonised your chi harmonisedand hydration to offset the year's heat and activity.

Tip: Balance is your medicine. Slow your pace, stay hydrated, and nourish your inner calm to keep Fire from overwhelming your system.

Symbolism of the Snake and Fire Horse

- The Snake symbolises wisdom, transformation, and intuition. It represents inner knowing, rebirth, and the ability to move gracefully through change.
- The Fire Horse symbolises vitality, independence, and freedom – it embodies motion, courage, and creative fire.

Together, they form a year of enlightened action – where intuition fuels inspired movement, and transformation happens from within. The Snake's calm intelligence tempers the Horse's impulsive flame, creating a balanced blend of passion and purpose.

Final Overview Tip for 2026

This is your year to evolve with grace. The Fire Horse invites you to move, grow, and shine – but to do so with mindfulness and poise. Trust your intuition, speak thoughtfully, and align your heart with your higher purpose. When inner stillness meets outer action, the results are transformative.

MAY, Flying Star 5: A Star of Dark Omens and Harbingers of Misfortune

In May, the menacing energy of Flying Star 5 reclaims the spotlight, weaving its way into the intricate tapestry of cosmic influences. Known as the infamous 5 Yellow Star, this celestial force casts a foreboding shadow over all it touches. It is one of the most treacherous and aggressive stars in Feng Shui, renowned for ushering in danger, misfortune, and disruptive forces. The reputation of Flying Star 5 precedes it—a harbinger of woes, a bringer of bad luck, and a weaver of calamities.

As this ominous star unfurls its dark energy, it sets the stage for adversity and hindrances, spreading its evil influence across all aspects of life. Its toxic aura attracts unfavourable outcomes, with the middle-aged women and daughters and those born under the Horse zodiac signs particularly vulnerable to its pernicious effects. The misfortunes it brings are vast and disheartening, ranging from financial loss and business disruptions to betrayals, tragic accidents, and even fatal calamities.

A palpable sense of dread surrounds Flying Star 5, as it embodies an array of negative energies that can envelop one's endeavours in a shroud of despair. This star symbolises bankruptcy, disloyalty, and other harbingers of doom that threaten to topple even the most stable foundations.

Ancient Feng Shui wisdom offers valuable guidance to guard against its ominous influence. Breaking ground or initiating new renovation projects under this star's presence is strongly discouraged, as it may unleash its potent negativity. The most effective strategy is to let this star lie dormant and undisturbed, minimising interaction with its energy. However, when avoidance isn't possible, remedies can be employed to mitigate its effects. The Brass Pagoda, the solemn tones of a bronze bell, the harmonious melody of metal wind chimes, and the purifying Saltwater Cure all serve as potent countermeasures. Additionally, invoking the benevolent presence of Ganesha, the remover of obstacles, can provide solace and protection.

To further counteract the grip of this adversarial star, strategically place heavy metal objects made of brass, copper, bronze, or pewter in the South sector of the home. Incorporating metallic artwork, decor, and colours that resonate with resistance can help diminish its influence. Simultaneously, minimising Fire and Earth energies in this area will weaken its potency, ensuring a safer and more harmonious environment during the star's reign.

In 2026, the annual Flying Star 5 will undermine the South sector of the Luo Shu (Bagua) School of Feng Shui, a domain traditionally associated with fame, recognition, and reputation. The Fire element governs this sector and is symbolically represented by the celestial red phoenix.

Enhancing your home's southern area to harness this sector's potent energies is advantageous. This can be achieved by strategically using the Phoenix statue or imagery of horses, which embody the speed and endurance essential for success. Embracing bright lighting and incorporating red or fire-coloured objects will amplify the sector's influence. Additionally, integrating wood elements, such as plants, will harmonise the interaction between water and fire energies, fostering a balanced environment. Including galloping horse symbols is particularly effective, as it invigorates your pursuits and motivates you to achieve recognition and acclaim throughout 2026.

Refer to page 12 for this month flying star chart

05 | MAY 2026

The Fire Horse Year

7 Thursday
Animal: **Metal Snake**
Flying Star: **3**
Good Day: **Monkey**
Bad Day: **Pig**

8 Friday
Animal: **Water Horse**
Flying Star: **4**
Good Day: **Goat**
Bad Day: **Rat**

9 Saturday
Animal: **Water Goat**
Flying Star: **5**
Good Day: **Horse**
Bad Day: **Ox**

10 Sunday
Animal: **Wood Monkey**
Flying Star: **6**
Good Day: **Snake**
Bad Day: **Tiger**

11 Monday
Animal: **Wood Rooster**
Flying Star: **7**
Good Day: **Dragon**
Bad Day: **Rabbit**

12 Tuesday
Animal: **Fire Dog**
Flying Star: **8**
Good Day: **Rabbit**
Bad Day: **Dragon**

13 Wednesday
Animal: **Fire Pig**
Flying Star: **9**
Good Day: **Tiger**
Bad Day: **Snake**

MAY MONTHLY 2026 CHINESE ZODIAC OVERVIEW

RAT

Emotions may run high as energy fluctuations make you more reactive than usual. Ground yourself before responding to challenges. For those ready for change, career or location shifts may bring long-term benefits. In relationships, patience and honest communication will prevent unnecessary tension.

OX

Change is in the air, and the month may bring shifts in plans or direction. Stay open-minded and don't resist what's evolving. In competitive settings, be cautious of false promises or deals that seem too good to be true. Focus on self-care and mental grounding – inner stability will guide you through outer change.

TIGER

Momentum builds, and productivity peaks. You'll find it easier to complete projects and maintain focus. Financial prospects are favourable, and your persistence begins to yield visible results. However, tension may surface in relationships – choose understanding over reaction. Patience and empathy are your keys to smoother interactions.

RABBIT

A dynamic and progressive month for business development and career growth. Productivity peaks, and financial prospects strengthen. It's an excellent time to launch projects, expand connections, and take inspired action. Social life flourishes, especially for singles – new and exciting people may enter your orbit, bringing joy and possibility.

DRAGON

A brighter, more supportive energy returns. Cooperation from others improves, and you'll feel a renewed sense of confidence and direction. Past worries begin to ease, and life regains its balance. Take time off or enjoy a short getaway to recharge. Emotional connection deepens through presence and quality time – harmony grows where appreciation is shown.

SNAKE

Energy fluctuations persist, urging you to stay centred and composed. Maintain a positive outlook and motivation despite changing circumstances. Financial vigilance is essential, especially when handling large transactions or agreements. Keep communication transparent and decisions grounded in logic rather than emotion.

05 | MAY 2026

The Fire Horse Year

14 Thursday
Animal: **Earth Rat**
Flying Star: **1**
Good Day: **Ox**
Bad Day: **Horse**

15 Friday
Animal: **Earth Ox**
Flying Star: **2**
Good Day: **Rat**
Bad Day: **Goat**

16 Saturday
Animal: **Metal Tiger**
Flying Star: **3**
Good Day: **Pig**
Bad Day: **Monkey**

17 Sunday
Animal: **Metal Rabbit**
Flying Star: **4**
Good Day: **Dog**
Bad Day: **Rooster**

18 Monday
Animal: **Water Dragon**
Flying Star: **5**
Good Day: **Rooster**
Bad Day: **Dog**

19 Tuesday
Animal: **Water Snake**
Flying Star: **6**
Good Day: **Monkey**
Bad Day: **Pig**

20 Wednesday
Animal: **Wood Horse**
Flying Star: **7**
Good Day: **Goat**
Bad Day: **Rat**

HORSE

Energy fluctuates, testing your focus and inner calm. Avoid scattering your attention or taking on too much at once. Stay grounded in the present and complete your current commitments before starting new ventures. Emotionally, steer clear of unnecessary conflicts. Financially, exercise caution and avoid impulsive spending or speculative risks.

GOAT

An intense, fast-paced month demands focus and determination. Workloads may increase, and it's easy to feel stretched thin – pace yourself. Avoid major life or career changes until energy stabilises. Relationships require extra patience and understanding to avoid misunderstandings. Stay grounded and conserve energy where possible.

MONKEY

A bright, motivating month that supports action and confidence. Career goals and personal ambitions are well-defined, allowing you to move forward decisively. Financial luck is stable with potential small gains. A short getaway or time in nature will refresh your mind and spark new insights. A joyful and productive month overall.

ROOSTER

A bright, fast-paced month brings opportunity and excitement. Work and business activities thrive, while social life blossoms. Singles may meet someone intriguing, though new relationships will need time to deepen. Amid the busyness, balance is essential – remember to prioritise rest, hydration, and good routines to sustain your momentum.

DOG

A bright, optimistic month filled with forward momentum. Career prospects strengthen, and achievements come within reach. If you've been considering a change in direction, this is a favourable time to take decisive, well-planned action. Wealth energy is supportive – you are entering a lucky phase where consistency and courage bring results.

PIG

A dynamic, invigorating month filled with potential breakthroughs. The energy encourages you to let go of outdated habits and welcome positive change. Health and vitality remain stable, especially when you balance work commitments with fun and leisure. Embrace opportunities with calm confidence – this is your time to evolve and grow beyond your comfort zone.

05 | MAY 2026

The Fire Horse Year

21 Thursday
Animal: **Wood Goat**
Flying Star: **8**
Good Day: **Horse**
Bad Day: **Ox**

22 Friday
Animal: **Fire Monkey**
Flying Star: **9**
Good Day: **Snake**
Bad Day: **Tiger**

23 Saturday
Animal: **Fire Rooster**
Flying Star: **1**
Good Day: **Dragon**
Bad Day: **Rabbit**

24 Sunday
Animal: **Earth Dog**
Flying Star: **2**
Good Day: **Rabbit**
Bad Day: **Dragon**

25 Monday
Animal: **Earth Pig**
Flying Star: **3**
Good Day: **Tiger**
Bad Day: **Snake**

26 Tuesday
Animal: **Metal Rat**
Flying Star: **4**
Good Day: **Ox**
Bad Day: **Horse**

27 Wednesday
Animal: **Metal Ox**
Flying Star: **5**
Good Day: **Goat**
Bad Day: **Rat**

05 | MAY 2026

The Fire Horse Year

28 Thursday
Animal: **Water Tiger**
Flying Star: **6**
Good Day: **Pig**
Bad Day: **Monkey**

29 Friday
Animal: **Water Rabbit**
Flying Star: **7**
Good Day: **Dog**
Bad Day: **Rooster**

30 Saturday
Animal: **Wood Dragon**
Flying Star: **8**
Good Day: **Rooster**
Bad Day: **Dog**

31 Sunday
Animal: **Wood Snake**
Flying Star: **9**
Good Day: **Monkey**
Bad Day: **Pig**

1 Monday
Animal: **Fire Horse**
Flying Star: **1**
Good Day: **Goat**
Bad Day: **Rat**

2 Tuesday
Animal: **Fire Goat**
Flying Star: **2**
Good Day: **Horse**
Bad Day: **Ox**

3 Wednesday
Animal: **Earth Monkey**
Flying Star: **3**
Good Day: **Snake**
Bad Day: **Tiger**

June 6 – July 6 is the Month of the Horse

Horse Chinese Horoscope 2025: Embracing Passion and Adaptability

Horse Birth Years: 1918, 1930, 1942, 1954, 1966, 1978, 1990, 2002, 2014, 2026, 2038

HORSE – A Year of Transformation, Awakening, and Renewal in Your Own Fire Cycle

2026 is your ruling year – the Year of the Yang Fire Horse – and for those born under the sign of the Horse, it heralds a powerful cycle of change, awakening, and self-discovery. Yet, as with all self-penalty or "clashing" years, this period also carries both intensity and opportunity. You are riding in your own element, which means the energy is strong, fast, and magnified – but it must be managed wisely.

This is not a year to resist change; instead, it's a year to flow with it. Shifts, relocations, new beginnings, or sudden detours are all possible, yet each carries the seed of transformation. The Fire Horse's energy moves swiftly, and while it can unsettle, it also burns away stagnation and clears the path for renewal. By staying grounded, mindful, and adaptable, you can transform turbulence into triumph.

Career & Opportunities

Professionally, 2026 brings movement, expansion, and pivotal change. The clashing energy of your own sign may bring sudden shifts in direction – changes in leadership, relocation, or unexpected new opportunities. For many Horses, this can be the push needed to reinvent yourself or to pursue a long-delayed dream.

Your natural charisma and leadership ability will serve you well, but success this year depends on temperament and timing. Avoid impulsive decisions driven by emotion or ego; instead, plan strategically and evaluate opportunities from multiple angles before galloping forward.

The year favors adaptability, upskilling, and creative exploration. If you can remain flexible, 2026 becomes a launching pad for greater recognition and long-term advancement.

Tip: Think before you leap. Boldness wins, but only when guided by self-awareness and discipline.

Wealth & Prosperity

Financially, this is a year of potential and momentum, but it also requires careful handling. The Fire Horse amplifies prosperity opportunities – income growth, business expansion, or even sudden windfalls – yet the same fiery energy can lead to rash investments or overspending.

Keep emotions out of financial choices and avoid speculative ventures or "too good to be true" schemes. Instead, channel your energy into structured growth, long-term savings, and well-planned investments. If you stay steady and focused, the financial rewards of this year can be lasting and substantial.

Tip: Harness your ambition with control. Wealth grows strongest when guided by wisdom, not impulse.

Love & Relationships

As one of the Four Peach Blossom Stars, the Horse naturally attracts attention – and this year, your magnetic charm is especially potent. For singles, romance blooms easily. You may meet new and exciting partners, often through travel, work, or social events.

However, this same energy of attraction also brings temptation. Passion runs high, but so does restlessness. Boundaries, honesty, and integrity become essential, especially for those already in committed relationships. Misunderstandings or emotional flare-ups could surface if communication falters.

Couples who approach challenges with empathy and transparency will find the Fire Horse's influence rekindles passion and authenticity.

Tip: Let love be adventurous, but grounded. Honesty and loyalty are your anchors amid emotional fire.

Health & Well-being

With such an active and fast-moving year ahead, your well-being must be a top priority. The Fire Horse energy heightens both vitality and volatility – meaning you may feel bursts of energy followed by fatigue if you overexert yourself.

To stay balanced, maintain a consistent exercise routine, a balanced diet, and adequate rest. Avoid high-risk or extreme sports this year, as accidents and injuries are more likely under the self-clash influence. Practices that calm the nervous system – meditation, qigong, or gentle yoga – will help keep your chi harmonized and your mind clear.

Tip: Pace yourself. Strong energy must be guided, not exhausted. A calm Horse finishes the race stronger than a restless one.

Symbolism of the Horse and the Fire Horse

- The Horse symbolises freedom, progress, and vitality – the spirit of movement and self-expression.
- The Fire Horse, as a rare and potent configuration, amplifies passion, courage, and individuality – but also carries a volatile edge that must be managed with mindfulness.

When these two merge, the energy becomes both exhilarating and transformative – the perfect year for reinvention, self-mastery, and breaking through limitations. You are riding in your own element, where every challenge becomes an opportunity to refine your strength and wisdom.

Final Overview Tip for 2026

This is your year of powerful transformation. You are galloping through your own element, which means the pace is fast and emotions run high – but the rewards are equally great. Keep your focus, master your reactions, and stay grounded in humility. When you combine courage with calm, and passion with patience, you'll turn a clashing year into one of your most defining and empowering cycles yet.

JUNE, Flying Star 4: A Symphony of Romance, Wisdom, and Scholarly Flourish

In June, the celestial energies align to bring forth the harmonious influence of Flying Star 4, a beacon of romance, wisdom, and intellectual brilliance. Emerging as a graceful melody within the cosmic symphony, this star weaves an intricate tapestry of love, intelligence, talent, and scholarly achievement. Known as the Peach Blossom Star, Flying Star 4 radiates beauty and knowledge, enriching the lives of those it touches and infusing the environment with grace and charm.

As the energies of Flying Star 4 permeate your surroundings, love and relationships take on an enchanting glow. Its benevolent presence nurtures meaningful connections, fostering harmony and happiness in romantic endeavours. This star promises love blossoming and deepening emotional bonds, which is exceptionally favourable for those born under the Ox and Tiger signs, as well as for the youngest son. For singles, it offers the prospect of finding a soulmate, while couples find their connection strengthened under its gentle influence.

Beyond the realm of the heart, Flying Star 4 extends its blessings to those with artistic, literary, or intellectual pursuits. Educators, artists, writers, and researchers are poised to benefit from its favourable energies, opening doors to advancement, recognition, and new opportunities. Students, too, find themselves under its protective wing, enjoying better exam results and tremendous success in academic endeavours. The star's touch enhances creativity and intellect, making it a powerful ally for those seeking wisdom and scholarly achievement.

To amplify this star's romantic energy, couples are encouraged to adorn their spaces with symbols of love. Placing two Rose Quartz crystals near the bed invokes the power of affection and harmony. At the same time, love symbols such as Mandarin Ducks, Wish-fulfilling Birds, or embracing figurines remind us of the tender connection between partners.

For those seeking academic success, Flying Star 4 offers a guiding light. Displaying Chinese ink brushes, artistic creations, tiered pagodas, or symbols of revered figures like the Chinese saint Luohan or the three Star Gods can help harmonise with the star's essence. These tokens act as conduits, channelling the star's energy to illuminate the path to academic excellence and intellectual growth.

In June, Flying Star 4 invites you to embrace its gifts of love, wisdom, and creativity, transforming your environment into a sanctuary of romance and scholarly brilliance.

In 2026, the Northeast sector of the Luo Shu, or Bagua, School of Feng Shui holds great significance, as it hosts the annual Flying Star 5, a symbol of knowledge, scholarly pursuits, learning, and education. This presents a prime opportunity for Feng Shui adjustments that could usher in positive transformations in these areas, instilling homeowners with renewed hope and optimism.

The Northeast, governed by the Earth element, balances and harnesses its potential. To support this sector, consider incorporating imagery of mountains, a crystal globe, a world map, the Chinese saint Luohan, or Dragon Carp. These elements can enhance and support the area's energy. Additionally, be mindful of any large trees or gaps that might obstruct this sector, as addressing these issues will be crucial to tapping into its full potential. Your deliberate efforts can significantly influence your home's energy and its impact on your life.

Refer to page 12 for this month flying star chart

06 JUNE 2026

The Fire Horse Year

4 Thursday
Animal: **Earth Rooster**
Flying Star: **4**
Good Day: **Dragon**
Bad Day: **Rabbit**

❤️ 🏠

5 Friday
Animal: **Metal Dog**
Flying Star: **5**
Good Day: **Rabbit**
Bad Day: **Dragon**

⚡ ✈️ 🔪 🏠

6 Saturday
Animal: **Metal Pig**
Flying Star: **6**
Good Day: **Tiger**
Bad Day: **Snake**

🎬 ✈️ 🏠

7 Sunday
Animal: **Water Rat**
Flying Star: **7**
Good Day: **Ox**
Bad Day: **Horse**

8 Monday
Animal: **Water Ox**
Flying Star: **8**
Good Day: **Rat**
Bad Day: **Goat**

🎬 🎉 🔪

9 Tuesday
Animal: **Wood Tiger**
Flying Star: **9**
Good Day: **Pig**
Bad Day: **Monkey**

🎬 🎉 🔪

10 Wednesday
Animal: **Wood Rabbit**
Flying Star: **1**
Good Day: **Dog**
Bad Day: **Rooster**

JUNE MONTHLY 2026 CHINESE ZODIAC OVERVIEW

RAT

A brighter, more joyful vibration surrounds you. It's a social month filled with laughter, gatherings, and renewed enthusiasm for life. Singles could attract new admirers, while couples rekindle closeness. Professionally, creativity flows easily – use this time to review your achievements and refine your next steps.

OX

This month's energy carries a mix of strength and stubbornness. Trying to control outcomes can lead to frustration; flow with life's rhythm instead of resisting it. Relationships will smooth out through patience and empathy. Financially, keep things steady and practical–adaptability and kindness open new pathways to harmony.

TIGER

A testing month for your determination and flexibility. Some projects may stall or take unexpected turns, but don't lose faith. Prioritise what truly aligns with your goals and let go of distractions. On the personal front, nurture your closest relationships with care – they will provide comfort and grounding amid shifting tides.

RABBIT

Energetic fluctuations may create tension or misunderstandings. Demands from others may feel heavier, so maintain clear, mindful communication. Stay focused on completing existing work rather than starting too many new tasks. Spending quality time with loved ones helps restore harmony and inner calm.

DRAGON

With energy intensifying, consistency in routine becomes vital. Maintain your health through balanced habits, and manage stress with physical activity or mindfulness practices. Not everyone will be ready for your new ideas – allow others time to adjust. Shared interests or light-hearted activities with loved ones will help ease tension and nurture closeness.

SNAKE

Unpredictability continues to shape this month. Workplace changes or shifting dynamics call for adaptability and teamwork. Avoid confrontation and remain cooperative to achieve the best results. Be cautious with investments – patience and prudence are key. Prioritise health through rest, mindful eating, and regular exercise to sustain your energy.

06 | JUNE 2026

The Fire Horse Year

11 Thursday
Animal: **Fire Dragon**
Flying Star: **2**
Good Day: **Rooster**
Bad Day: **Dog**

12 Friday
Animal: **Fire Snake**
Flying Star: **3**
Good Day: **Monkey**
Bad Day: **Pig**

13 Saturday
Animal: **Earth Horse**
Flying Star: **4**
Good Day: **Goat**
Bad Day: **Rat**
❤️

14 Sunday
Animal: **Earth Goat**
Flying Star: **5**
Good Day: **Horse**
Bad Day: **Ox**

15 Monday
Animal: **Metal Monkey**
Flying Star: **6**
Good Day: **Snake**
Bad Day: **Tiger**

16 Tuesday
Animal: **Metal Rooster**
Flying Star: **7**
Good Day: **Dragon**
Bad Day: **Rabbit**

17 Wednesday
Animal: **Water Dog**
Flying Star: **8**
Good Day: **Rabbit**
Bad Day: **Dragon**

HORSE

A slower pace brings the opportunity to refine your direction. Delays may occur, but they serve a higher purpose: helping you reassess your priorities. Take time for rest and reflection; connect with nature or activities that soothe the spirit. Emotional overthinking may drain you, so stay light and trust the process. Clarity will return when you allow space for it.

GOAT

This fast-moving month can be both productive and draining. Your schedule may fill quickly, leaving little room for rest. Guard your emotional well-being and avoid reacting impulsively to sudden changes. Keep your plans flexible and refrain from making big decisions under pressure – simplicity and calm will prevent unnecessary complications.

MONKEY

A powerful yet demanding energy dominates this month. You may feel stretched or mentally fatigued as work accelerates. Maintain structure through mindfulness, rest, and healthy routines. Consistent focus and discipline will help you meet expectations without losing balance. Remember – steady progress outperforms haste.

ROOSTER

Renewed support arrives, lifting your motivation and optimism. Work matters run more smoothly, and new opportunities begin to emerge. Maintain steady discipline and guard your health through balanced living – mindful eating, regular rest, and time for relaxation will enhance both focus and well-being—a rewarding month for consistent effort.

DOG

This month's shifting energy may bring sudden changes or surprises. Adaptability and focus are essential to stay on track. Simplify your workload and prioritise what truly matters. Unexpected developments may challenge routines, but by staying calm and flexible, you'll turn them into valuable growth opportunities.

PIG

Vibrant energy fuels motivation and progress. You may find yourself busier than usual, but this pace helps refine your goals and highlight your strengths. Sudden opportunities for career advancement or recognition could appear – trust your instincts and act with clarity. Collaborations and partnerships bring excellent results when grounded in mutual respect.

06 | JUNE 2026

The Fire Horse Year

18 Thursday
Animal: **Water Pig**
Flying Star: **9**
Good Day: **Tiger**
Bad Day: **Snake**

19 Friday
Animal: **Wood Rat**
Flying Star: **1**
Good Day: **Ox**
Bad Day: **Horse**

20 Saturday
Animal: **Wood Ox**
Flying Star: **2**
Good Day: **Rat**
Bad Day: **Goat**

21 Sunday
Animal: **Fire Tiger**
Flying Star: **3/4**
Good Day: **Pig**
Bad Day: **Monkey**

22 Monday
Animal: **Fire Rabbit**
Flying Star: **3**
Good Day: **Dog**
Bad Day: **Rooster**

23 Tuesday
Animal: **Earth Dragon**
Flying Star: **2**
Good Day: **Rooster**
Bad Day: **Dog**

24 Wednesday
Animal: **Earth Snake**
Flying Star: **1**
Good Day: **Monkey**
Bad Day: **Pig**

06 | JUNE 2026

The Fire Horse Year

25 Thursday
- Animal: **Metal Horse**
- Flying Star: **9**
- Good Day: **Goat**
- Bad Day: **Rat**

26 Friday
- Animal: **Metal Goat**
- Flying Star: **8**
- Good Day: **Horse**
- Bad Day: **Ox**

27 Saturday
- Animal: **Water Monkey**
- Flying Star: **7**
- Good Day: **Snake**
- Bad Day: **Tiger**

28 Sunday
- Animal: **Water Rooster**
- Flying Star: **6**
- Good Day: **Dragon**
- Bad Day: **Rabbit**

29 Monday
- Animal: **Wood Dog**
- Flying Star: **5**
- Good Day: **Rabbit**
- Bad Day: **Dragon**

30 Tuesday
- Animal: **Wood Pig**
- Flying Star: **4**
- Good Day: **Tiger**
- Bad Day: **Snake**

1 Wednesday
- Animal: **Fire Rat**
- Flying Star: **3**
- Good Day: **Ox**
- Bad Day: **Horse**

July 7 – August 7 is the Month of the Goat

Goat Chinese Horoscope 2025: Flourishing with the Fire Snake

Goat Birth Years: 1919, 1931, 1943, 1955, 1967, 1979, 1991, 2003, 2015, 2027, 2039

GOAT – A Year of Harmony, Fulfilment, and Gentle Prosperity in the Fire Horse Cycle

In 2026, the Yang Fire Horse shines brightly upon the gentle and artistic Goat, marking one of the most harmonious alignments in the Chinese zodiac. This year can bring joy, fulfilment, and steady advancement across multiple areas of your life. The dynamic energy of the Horse complements your kind-hearted and graceful nature, offering motivation and forward movement without the turbulence that other signs may experience.

Surrounding your sign are auspicious stars radiating positivity and divine support, helping you attract the right people, opportunities, and experiences. Whether in personal or professional realms, you'll feel guided and uplifted – a sense that life is finally aligning in your favour. Still, harmony does not mean idleness. The key to success lies in balancing enjoyment with discipline, compassion with self-care, and creativity with structure.

Career & Opportunities

This year holds promise for progress, recognition, and fruitful collaboration. The Fire Horse's energy infuses your professional world with movement and visibility. You may experience growth in influence, a new project, or advancement within your field, especially if your work involves creativity, healing, education, or people-oriented roles.

Your diplomatic and cooperative nature will be your strongest asset – you have a unique ability to smooth conflicts and create harmony in team settings. Challenges may appear in the form of workload pressure or competitive colleagues, but your tact and patience will see you through. The year also favours networking and partnership, so reach out, connect, and expand your circle.

Tip: Be confident in your quiet strength. Progress may come softly but steadily – each step, thoughtfully taken, leads to long-term success.

Wealth & Prosperity

While 2026 is generally favourable, the Fire Horse's active energy can sometimes tempt the indulgent Goat toward overspending. Your appreciation for comfort, art, and beauty may lead to unnecessary expenses, so this is a year to adopt financial mindfulness.

Income remains stable, and potential gains are possible through collaboration or steady business expansion, particularly in creative, design, or wellness-related industries. However, for those in retail or self-employment, market fluctuations or increased competition may require strategic planning and prudent budgeting. Keep reserves for unexpected costs and avoid speculative ventures.

Tip: Practice elegant restraint. Save before you spend, and let financial stability be your foundation for future comfort and joy.

Love & Relationships

Relationships and social connections flourish under the harmonious energy between the Goat and the Horse. This is a relationship-friendly year, rich in opportunities for love, companionship, and emotional fulfilment.

Singles will find themselves more magnetic and sociable than usual, attracting new and exciting relationships through social events, networking, or creative pursuits. For those in committed relationships, this is the perfect year to rekindle romance, plan shared adventures, or strengthen emotional bonds through kindness and communication.

This energy also enhances family relationships and friendships, encouraging heartfelt exchanges and stronger community ties. Just be mindful of overextending yourself emotionally – balance care for others with time for self-renewal.

Tip: Love and harmony bloom when you nurture a connection without losing yourself. Prioritise both giving and receiving equally.

Health & Well-being

Your well-being remains generally strong this year, though moderation is key. The Fire Horse's vibrant pace may pull you into overactivity or indulgence, leading to fatigue if boundaries are not maintained. Pay attention to blood pressure, stomach, and kidney function, especially if you have pre-existing sensitivities.

Balance work with rest, and avoid excessive stress by maintaining a calming routine. Gentle physical activities such as yoga, stretching, or nature walks will harmonise your chi and sustain energy. Remember – serenity is your power source.

Tip: Listen to your body's whispers before they become shouts. Maintain equilibrium through rest, hydration, and mindful self-care.

Symbolism of the Goat and Fire Horse

- The Goat symbolises compassion, artistry, and inner peace. It represents creativity, empathy, and the gentle strength that heals and unites.
- The Fire Horse symbolises vitality, courage, and freedom – its energy ignites motivation, inspiration, and action.

Together, this pairing creates a beautiful synergy of grace and momentum. The Goat's calm, nurturing nature softens the Horse's fiery speed, creating a year where sensitivity meets strength, and dreams find tangible form.

Final Overview Tip for 2026

This is your year to flow with joy and balance. The universe supports your growth, creativity, and emotional fulfilment, but it asks for mindfulness in spending, self-care, and time management. By blending your gentle wisdom with the Fire Horse's enthusiasm, you'll create a year of harmony, abundance, and graceful success.

JULY Flying Star 3, Discord, Conflict, and Caution

July brings a cloud of discord as Flying Star 3 makes its ominous entrance into the celestial ballet. This star brings a surge of turbulent energies, vibrating with the unsettling resonance of conflict and strife. However, it's important to remember that there is potential for positive change even amid this turbulence. In its wake, seeds of gossip, disputes, and legal challenges find fertile ground, sprouting into full-blown turmoil. Far from benign, Flying Star 3 is a force of hostility, notorious for weaving a complex tapestry of violence, anger, and endless disagreements. It heralds a storm of misunderstandings, igniting fiery arguments and even litigation, casting a dark shadow over relationships between family members, friends, and colleagues.

The health ramifications that accompany this star are equally foreboding. It targets the liver, gallbladder, and the feet and arms, manifesting as physical discomfort and malaise. As its influence spreads, productivity may falter, with the atmosphere thickening under the weight of conflict and friction.

Particularly vulnerable are those born in the Year of the Rooster and the youngest daughter of the household. Marital bonds and familial harmony become entangled in the web of Flying Star 3's disruptive energies. The tension it fosters can cast a long shadow over relationships between spouses, eroding the foundations of family stability and marriage. The looming threat of conflict with authorities and potential legal entanglements is a stark reminder of the need for heightened caution during this period. It's crucial to be alert and prepared, as this caution can help us navigate the challenges of Flying Star 3 with resilience and strength.

Under the influence of Flying Star 3, July calls for a vigilant, defensive approach. However, it's important to remember that various remedies can counteract its negative energy. The traditional Chinese cure—a simple red piece of paper—can be a powerful tool to ward off its malign influence. Surroundings can be imbued with the protective energies of red and purple, introduced through decor, candles, and bright lights. The magic flaming wheel, a symbolic shield, can also be invoked to fend off negativity. Images of the fiery red phoenix or the watchful eagle can be guardians, defending against discord. For those seeking an extra layer of protection, the steadfast presence of temple lions and the vigilant gaze of the evil eye symbol can be enlisted to keep the darkness at bay. These remedies offer a beacon of hope, empowering us to navigate the challenges of Flying Star 3 with resilience and strength.

In 2026, the Western sector of the Luo Shu or Bagua School of Feng Shui will be significantly strained. This sector, marked by the annual Flying Star 3, embodies the themes of family, descendants, and safeguarding wealth and assets. This insight enables strategic Feng Shui adjustments, giving you the foresight to prepare and enhance your environment for the year ahead.

The Western sector is the domain of the celestial white Tiger, making it vital to incorporate Tiger symbolism here to fortify and protect family luck. In this area, place wealth-related symbols such as Gold Coins, Gold Ingots, or a Wealth God to bolster wealth and ensure the family's well-being. The Western sector is associated with the Metal element, so integrating metallic artwork, paintings, or colours, as well as displaying family photos in metallic frames, will harmonise and enhance the energy of this space.

Refer to page 12 for this month flying star chart

07 | JULY
2026

The Fire Horse Year

2
Thursday

Animal: **Fire Ox**
Flying Star: **2**
Good Day: **Rat**
Bad Day: **Goat**

3
Friday

Animal: **Earth Tiger**
Flying Star: **1**
Good Day: **Pig**
Bad Day: **Monkey**

4
Saturday

Animal: **Earth Rabbit**
Flying Star: **9**
Good Day: **Dog**
Bad Day: **Rooster**

5
Sunday

Animal: **Metal Dragon**
Flying Star: **8**
Good Day: **Rooster**
Bad Day: **Dog**

6
Monday

Animal: **Metal Snake**
Flying Star: **7**
Good Day: **Monkey**
Bad Day: **Pig**

7
Tuesday

Animal: **Water Horse**
Flying Star: **6**
Good Day: **Goat**
Bad Day: **Rat**

8
Wednesday

Animal: **Water Goat**
Flying Star: **5**
Good Day: **Horse**
Bad Day: **Ox**

JULY MONTHLY 2026 CHINESE ZODIAC OVERVIEW

RAT

A strong, supportive month that amplifies your confidence and magnetism. People respond well to your ideas, and your leadership qualities shine. Financially stable energy prevails, yet balance your work commitments with rest. Your well-being remains your greatest asset – nurture it.

OX

A contemplative month that invites you to review your goals and long-term plans. Even if progress feels slower, trust that you are aligning with your greater purpose. Health and vitality improve through consistent routines – movement, mindfulness, and nature will uplift your spirit. Short trips bring refreshment and perspective.

TIGER

Stability returns as your focus sharpens and energy steadies. Opportunities in career or business arise unexpectedly – be ready to act when they do. Financial flow remains steady, though prudence in spending is still advised. Keep your mindset optimistic; it's your magnet for success this month.

RABBIT

The month ushers in renewed positivity and flow. Challenges ease, and pending issues can be resolved with greater ease and clarity. Finances remain stable, and it's an auspicious time to begin new projects or collaborations. Expect your social and professional calendars to fill – balance activity with time for self-care.

DRAGON

A fluctuating month that may leave you feeling both inspired and fatigued. Protect your vitality with regular rest and grounding rituals. Financial stability remains average – avoid stretching your resources. This is a good time to consolidate gains, focus on stability, and nurture your inner resilience rather than push forward too aggressively.

SNAKE

A surge of supportive energy revitalises your confidence and drive. Optimism grows, and this is an excellent time to act on plans or launch new ideas. Job seekers and business owners alike may see promising opportunities. Maintain balance by carving out time for leisure, grounding practices, and time outdoors to replenish your vitality.

HORSE

Home, relationships, and personal well-being take precedence this month. Tend to what truly matters and address unfinished matters at home or within close relationships. While the energy feels calmer, it may also bring moments of

07 | **JULY 2026**

The Fire Horse Year

9
Thursday

Animal: **Wood Monkey**
Flying Star: **4**
Good Day: **Snake**
Bad Day: **Tiger**

10
Friday

Animal: **Wood Rooster**
Flying Star: **3**
Good Day: **Dragon**
Bad Day: **Rabbit**

11
Saturday

Animal: **Fire Dog**
Flying Star: **2**
Good Day: **Rabbit**
Bad Day: **Dragon**

12
Sunday

Animal: **Fire Pig**
Flying Star: **1**
Good Day: **Tiger**
Bad Day: **Snake**

13
Monday

Animal: **Earth Rat**
Flying Star: **9**
Good Day: **Ox**
Bad Day: **Horse**

14
Tuesday

Animal: **Earth Ox**
Flying Star: **8**
Good Day: **Rat**
Bad Day: **Goat**

15
Wednesday

Animal: **Metal Tiger**
Flying Star: **7**
Good Day: **Pig**
Bad Day: **Monkey**

restlessness. Financially, small but steady gains are indicated. Move gently and focus on nurturing stability rather than chasing outcomes.

GOAT

Activity continues at a brisk pace, but now you have more clarity. Avoid taking on extra responsibilities or volunteering for tasks outside your capacity. Those seeking new career directions may find promising leads now. Financial energy is balanced, though careful expense management remains essential. Prioritise rest to keep your energy vibrant.

MONKEY

Momentum stabilises, and progress continues at a measured pace. Unexpected disruptions may occur, but they won't derail your path if you stay composed. Family and social support will help you maintain optimism. Prioritise health through exercise, balanced nutrition, and grounding activities – these will sustain your energy and clarity.

ROOSTER

A bright and favourable month filled with vitality. Progress and recognition are likely, and finances remain strong, with the possibility of bonuses or additional income. Confidence draws positive attention, making this an excellent time for networking and collaboration. Love energy also shines – whether single or partnered, relationships deepen with warmth and harmony.

DOG

Diplomacy and flexibility are crucial this month. People around you may be more reactive or demanding, so approach situations with patience and calm communication. Compromise leads to smoother relationships and a more peaceful atmosphere. Gentle exercise, mindfulness, and time outdoors will keep you centred and energised.

PIG

Supportive energy continues to flow, boosting confidence and enthusiasm. Career and business matters expand steadily, and your consistent effort will be rewarded. Wealth energy is intense, with opportunities for extra income or small gains through projects and investments. Family life feels joyful and celebratory – news or events may bring happiness to your household.

07 | JULY 2026

The Fire Horse Year

16 Thursday
Animal: **Metal Rabbit**
Flying Star: **6**
Good Day: **Dog**
Bad Day: **Rooster**

17 Friday
Animal: **Water Dragon**
Flying Star: **5**
Good Day: **Rooster**
Bad Day: **Dog**

18 Saturday
Animal: **Water Snake**
Flying Star: **4**
Good Day: **Monkey**
Bad Day: **Pig**

19 Sunday
Animal: **Wood Horse**
Flying Star: **3**
Good Day: **Goat**
Bad Day: **Rat**

20 Monday
Animal: **Wood Goat**
Flying Star: **2**
Good Day: **Horse**
Bad Day: **Ox**

21 Tuesday
Animal: **Fire Monkey**
Flying Star: **1**
Good Day: **Snake**
Bad Day: **Tiger**

22 Wednesday
Animal: **Fire Rooster**
Flying Star: **9**
Good Day: **Dragon**
Bad Day: **Rabbit**

07 | JULY 2026

The Fire Horse Year

23 Thursday
Animal: **Earth Dog**
Flying Star: **8**
Good Day: **Rabbit**
Bad Day: **Dragon**

24 Friday
Animal: **Earth Pig**
Flying Star: **7**
Good Day: **Tiger**
Bad Day: **Snake**

25 Saturday
Animal: **Metal Rat**
Flying Star: **6**
Good Day: **Ox**
Bad Day: **Horse**

26 Sunday
Animal: **Metal Ox**
Flying Star: **5**
Good Day: **Rat**
Bad Day: **Goat**

27 Monday
Animal: **Water Tiger**
Flying Star: **4**
Good Day: **Pig**
Bad Day: **Monkey**

28 Tuesday
Animal: **Water Rabbit**
Flying Star: **3**
Good Day: **Dog**
Bad Day: **Rooster**

29 Wednesday
Animal: **Wood Dragon**
Flying Star: **2**
Good Day: **Rooster**
Bad Day: **Dog**

August 8 – September 7 is the Month of the Monkey

Monkey Chinese Horoscope 2025: Embracing Transformation and Passion

Monkey Birth Years: 1920, 1932, 1944, 1956, 1968, 1980, 1992, 2004, 2016, 2028, 2040

MONKEY – A Year of Reflection, Refinement, and Subtle Progress in the Fire Horse Cycle

For those born under the clever and quick-witted sign of the Monkey, the Yang Fire Horse year of 2026 brings a dynamic yet delicate balance between movement and moderation. This is a year of mixed blessings – moments of restlessness intertwined with opportunities for inner refinement. While your sign does not clash with the ruling Horse, the fiery pace of the year can ignite impatience, tempting you to act before the timing is ripe.

The Fire Horse energy moves swiftly, demanding courage and clarity, yet the Monkey's true success in 2026 will come through strategy, restraint, and preparation. You are naturally intelligent, resourceful, and innovative, but this is not a year for impulsive leaps. Instead, it's a time to fine-tune your plans, consolidate what you've built, and align your energy for the breakthroughs that await in the near future.

Career & Opportunities

Professionally, 2026 asks for adaptability and humility. The Fire Horse year can bring sudden shifts in team dynamics, leadership, or priorities, requiring you to think on your feet. Your ability to communicate, negotiate, and innovate will help you stay ahead – but only if paired with patience.

Avoid confrontations, unnecessary risks, or dramatic job changes driven by frustration. Progress will come through steady effort, tactful communication, and emotional intelligence. If you focus on improving your current projects, refining skills, and nurturing alliances, you'll find yourself well-positioned when the momentum turns in your favour later in the cycle.

Tip: The most brilliant move is not always the boldest one. This year, your power lies in patience, subtle influence, and consistent progress.

Wealth & Prosperity

Financially, 2026 encourages a steady, conservative approach. While your natural curiosity may draw you toward new ventures or speculative ideas, the energies of the year caution against risk-taking. Focus on strengthening existing income streams, paying down debts, and improving your long-term financial foundation.

Unexpected expenses could arise, particularly in travel or lifestyle choices, so budgeting and foresight are essential. This is also a good year to restructure finances, review investments, or seek expert advice for future growth. By staying grounded and methodical, your wealth can grow securely, if not dramatically.

Tip: Build quietly this year. Financial stability is your ladder to future success – climb it with patience, not haste.

Love & Relationships

In love, the Fire Horse year brings introspection and emotional lessons. For singles, relationships may take longer to form, or potential partners may not align with long-term goals. Don't be discouraged – these experiences are refining your understanding of what you truly need. Stay open, social, and genuine, and connections will gradually develop where energy aligns.

For those already in relationships, the key to harmony lies in communication and empathy. The fiery atmosphere of the year can heighten tempers or misunderstandings, but also rekindle passion when approached with care. Nurture your connection through patience and appreciation rather than expectation.

Tip: Love requires presence, not perfection. Slow down, listen deeply, and you'll rediscover warmth and emotional support.

Health & Well-being

Your mental and emotional health take center stage this year. The combination of Fire and movement can overstimulate the mind, leading to restlessness or fatigue if balance isn't maintained. Take time for self-reflection, grounding, and relaxation.

Creative outlets, travel, nature retreats, or meditation can help you reset and maintain clarity. Prioritize sleep and hydration, and avoid excessive screen time or multitasking. Keeping your nervous system calm will enhance focus, creativity, and overall vitality.

Tip: Balance activity with rest. A peaceful mind will amplify your brilliance and keep your chi flowing harmoniously throughout the year.

Symbolism of the Monkey and Fire Horse

- The Monkey represents intelligence, adaptability, and wit – the sign of innovators and problem-solvers who thrive on curiosity and clever solutions.
- The Fire Horse embodies passion, freedom, and courage – a force of bold energy that propels movement and transformation.

Together, they create a year where mental agility meets fiery drive. But to benefit fully, the Monkey must temper speed with wisdom, ensuring that decisions are guided by clarity rather than impulse. When intellect leads and emotion follows, success becomes sustainable and deeply fulfilling.

Final Overview Tip for 2026

This is your year of refinement – to prepare, plan, and strengthen your inner and outer foundations. The Fire Horse pushes for action, but your power lies in pacing yourself and mastering timing. Approach life with patience, humor, and grace. By embracing calm determination over impulsive ambition, you'll turn restlessness into resilience and end the year stronger, wiser, and ready for the next leap forward.

AUGUST Flying Star 2: From Turmoil to Complex Energies

August ushers in the complex energies of Flying Star 2, a star that straddles both the remnants of its past and the promise of its future. As the cosmic dance continues, Star 2 takes place on the celestial stage, undergoing a profound metamorphosis that began in February 2024. While it now carries a glimmer of promising potential, the star's energy remains weak and still harbours the power of sickness and illness, a reminder of its turbulent legacy.

This transformation marks a significant shift in the cosmic landscape. Once a harbinger of affliction and negative energy during Period 8, Flying Star 2 is gradually shedding its inauspicious cloak as we progress into Period 9. Like a phoenix rising from the ashes, it embodies a new role as a force for positive change, although its influence remains cautious and tentative. Health and well-being, once threatened by this star, are now on the cusp of improvement, though the shadow of its past still lingers.

In Period 9, Flying Star 2 retains its Earth element, wielding energies that once wreaked havoc on health and peace. The early phases of this transition are marked by residual turbulence as the star's influence continues to present challenges, albeit less severe than in the past. Particularly vulnerable are those born in the Year of the Dog and Pig and the patriarch of the household.

For 2026, Star 2's presence is felt particularly if you have a Northwest entry, casting a subtle but undeniable influence on the lives of those it touches. While there may be opportunities in property and real estate endeavours, these gains could come at the expense of health. The toll may be paid through illness or physical discomfort, underscoring the need to manage this star's energy carefully.

To harness the transformative potential of Flying Star 2, a range of remedies is recommended. The Health Gourd, or Wu Lou, symbolises healing and well-being and is best accompanied by Six Gold Coins on a vibrant red tassel. A Saltwater Cure can help neutralise lingering negative energies, while the presence of Quan Yin invites benevolent vibrations into space. Wearing a Wu Lou pendant or amulet is a protective talisman, particularly for those with low life force energy, shielding them from the star's lingering effects.

Metal elements play a crucial role in counteracting the challenges posed by Flying Star 2. Brass, copper, bronze, and pewter objects, artworks, and decor items introduce stability and balance into the environment. Incorporating white, silver, and gold shades further harmonises the space with the star's evolving energy in Period 9, aligning interiors with its subtle yet significant transformation.

In 2026, the Northwest sector will be particularly significant for feng shui enhancements. According to the Luo Shu or Bagua School of Feng Shui, this area is governed by the annual Flying Star 2, which symbolises critical figures such as the man of the house, influential benefactors, mentors, and supportive individuals. Focusing on this sector can strengthen personal and professional relationships, encouraging and motivating homeowners.

The Northwest is associated with the Metal element, which, in Chinese culture, signifies gold and family wealth. To harness and amplify this energy, incorporate metal décor items, metallic objects, bells, or wind chimes. Additionally, placing the three Star Gods—representing health, wealth, and longevity—in the main living area can substantially benefit all household members, fostering a harmonious and prosperous environment.

Refer to page 12 for this month flying star chart

07 | JULY 2026

The Fire Horse Year

30 Thursday
- Animal: **Wood Snake**
- Flying Star: **1**
- Good Day: **Monkey**
- Bad Day: **Pig**

31 Friday
- Animal: **Fire Horse**
- Flying Star: **9**
- Good Day: **Goat**
- Bad Day: **Rat**

1 Saturday
- Animal: **Fire Goat**
- Flying Star: **8**
- Good Day: **Horse**
- Bad Day: **Ox**

2 Sunday
- Animal: **Earth Monkey**
- Flying Star: **7**
- Good Day: **Snake**
- Bad Day: **Tiger**

3 Monday
- Animal: **Earth Rooster**
- Flying Star: **6**
- Good Day: **Dragon**
- Bad Day: **Rabbit**

4 Tuesday
- Animal: **Metal Dog**
- Flying Star: **5**
- Good Day: **Rabbit**
- Bad Day: **Dragon**

5 Wednesday
- Animal: **Metal Pig**
- Flying Star: **4**
- Good Day: **Tiger**
- Bad Day: **Snake**

AUGUST MONTHLY 2026 CHINESE ZODIAC OVERVIEW

RAT

Life feels harmonious, and luck is on your side. Progress comes naturally, especially when working with a team or partnership. A perfect month to solidify plans or strengthen key relationships. If travelling, take precautions with your belongings and health – smooth energy depends on mindfulness.

OX

Fresh beginnings unfold, bringing momentum and opportunities to advance. Stay organised and proactive – momentum is your ally. Practical spending and grounded choices will ensure stability amid progress. Spend time outdoors to maintain energetic balance and reconnect with clarity and focus.

TIGER

An unpredictable month that calls for flexibility and mindfulness. Plans may change suddenly – adapt gracefully. Double-check details around travel or contracts, and be cautious when driving or engaging in physical activities. Stay centred and avoid rushing; balance and patience will keep you safe and productive.

RABBIT

After several busy months, the pace finally softens. Take this opportunity to reflect on your progress and identify where adjustments are needed to reach your goals. Financial energy is somewhat unstable – avoid risky ventures or impulsive purchases. Simplicity and mindfulness are your best guides now.

DRAGON

A productive and supportive period unfolds. Work and business flow positively, and wealth luck improves, making it a favourable month for refining long-term financial strategies. Maintain balance by pacing your commitments – overextending yourself can drain this otherwise auspicious energy. Harmony comes from structure and moderation.

SNAKE

A calmer, more stabilising influence brings balance after recent intensity. Collaboration and steady teamwork lead to progress, and strategic contracts or plans yield rewards. Financial energy remains stable. In relationships, heartfelt communication deepens trust and understanding. Gentle movement or light exercise will help maintain inner flow.

08 | AUGUST 2026

The Fire Horse Year

6 Thursday
Animal: **Water Rat**
Flying Star: **3**
Good Day: **Ox**
Bad Day: **Horse**

7 Friday
Animal: **Water Ox**
Flying Star: **2**
Good Day: **Rat**
Bad Day: **Goat**

8 Saturday
Animal: **Wood Tiger**
Flying Star: **1**
Good Day: **Pig**
Bad Day: **Monkey**

9 Sunday
Animal: **Wood Rabbit**
Flying Star: **9**
Good Day: **Dog**
Bad Day: **Rooster**

10 Monday
Animal: **Fire Dragon**
Flying Star: **8**
Good Day: **Rooster**
Bad Day: **Dog**

11 Tuesday
Animal: **Fire Snake**
Flying Star: **7**
Good Day: **Monkey**
Bad Day: **Pig**

12 Wednesday
Animal: **Fire Horse**
Flying Star: **6**
Good Day: **Goat**
Bad Day: **Rat**

HORSE

Momentum returns with bright, supportive energy. Obstacles lift, and progress resumes smoothly. This is an excellent month for finalising deals, launching projects, or taking action on long-term goals. Travel and new experiences will refresh your spirit. Social circles expand, offering fun and meaningful interactions – an uplifting month for love and opportunity.

GOAT

A refreshing and uplifting month brings helpful people into your life. Supportive alliances help you progress toward your goals with ease. Take advantage of this auspicious energy to set plans in motion and complete key projects. Toward the end of the month, minor relationship tensions may arise – patience and understanding will quickly restore peace.

MONKEY

A competitive yet rewarding month where ambition runs high. Your drive and determination will open new professional and financial doors. Success is best achieved through strategy, patience, and brilliant timing rather than force. Networking brings valuable opportunities, while mindfulness and relaxation help preserve emotional balance amid the hustle.

ROOSTER

Energy shifts, bringing fluctuations that test your flexibility. Sudden changes at work or within partnerships may require patience and careful handling. Avoid impulsive spending or risky financial ventures. Quiet reflection and balance are key – make time to nurture your emotional and spiritual well-being to stay aligned.

DOG

Patience and thoughtful communication are the keys to navigating this month's delicate energy. Work matters may move slowly, but progress is still being made behind the scenes. Financial stability continues, provided you avoid hasty decisions. In relationships, empathy and listening strengthen understanding and harmony.

PIG

A favourable and financially stable month. It's an ideal time to finalise plans, secure agreements, or launch key ventures. Positive money flow and supportive partnerships bring success. To sustain your momentum, maintain a balanced lifestyle – healthy nutrition, regular rest, and mindfulness will keep your body and mind in peak condition.

08 | AUGUST 2026

The Fire Horse Year

13 Thursday
Animal: **Earth Goat**
Flying Star: **5**
Good Day: **Horse**
Bad Day: **Ox**

⚡

14 Friday
Animal: **Earth Monkey**
Flying Star: **4**
Good Day: **Snake**
Bad Day: **Tiger**

✈️ ❤️

15 Saturday
Animal: **Metal Rooster**
Flying Star: **3**
Good Day: **Dragon**
Bad Day: **Rabbit**

🧰

16 Sunday
Animal: **Metal Dog**
Flying Star: **2**
Good Day: **Rabbit**
Bad Day: **Dragon**

🤵 💍 ✈️ 🏠

17 Monday
Animal: **Water Pig**
Flying Star: **1**
Good Day: **Tiger**
Bad Day: **Snake**

18 Tuesday
Animal: **Water Rat**
Flying Star: **9**
Good Day: **Ox**
Bad Day: **Horse**

✂️ 🧰 ✈️ 🏠

19 Wednesday
Animal: **Wood Ox**
Flying Star: **8**
Good Day: **Rat**
Bad Day: **Goat**

🧰

FENG SHUI PRINCIPLES FOR THE BEDROOM

The feng shui in your bedroom is of utmost importance, given that it's where you spend your most vulnerable and restorative hours. Tailoring feng shui principles to your style can enhance the overall energy and luck in your bedroom's decor.

Essential General Tips for the Bedroom:

Ensure your bedroom is of a regular shape, without missing corners, for balanced energy flow.

Keep plants and flowers out of the bedroom, as they can drain your energy, leaving you fatigued despite a good night's sleep.

Choose a bed that is the right size for you; one that is too small may hinder personal growth, while an overly large bed can contribute to relationship issues.

Opt for bedroom furniture with rounded edges and corners, avoiding overly angular designs to prevent the formation of harmful poison arrows that may lead to serious illness if left uncorrected.

Position the bed with the headboard against a wall, avoiding a "floating" arrangement in the centre of the bedroom.

Orient your bed to one of your auspicious directions for a more harmonious sleeping experience.

Minimise or avoid mirrors in the bedroom; place them inside a cabinet if necessary. Ensure that mirrors, especially those on dressing tables, do not face the bed directly, as exposed mirrors may invite interference in your relationships.

Choose neutral and relaxing colours for the bedroom to maintain a balanced energy. Avoid excessive Yang energy, which disrupts sleep patterns and keeps you awake at night.

08 | AUGUST 2026

The Fire Horse Year

20 Thursday
Animal: **Wood Tiger**
Flying Star: **7**
Good Day: **Pig**
Bad Day: **Monkey**

21 Friday
Animal: **Fire Rabbit**
Flying Star: **6**
Good Day: **Dog**
Bad Day: **Rooster**

22 Saturday
Animal: **Fire Dragon**
Flying Star: **5**
Good Day: **Rooster**
Bad Day: **Dog**

23 Sunday
Animal: **Earth Snake**
Flying Star: **4**
Good Day: **Monkey**
Bad Day: **Pig**

24 Monday
Animal: **Earth Horse**
Flying Star: **3**
Good Day: **Goat**
Bad Day: **Rat**

25 Tuesday
Animal: **Metal Goat**
Flying Star: **2**
Good Day: **Horse**
Bad Day: **Ox**

26 Wednesday
Animal: **Metal Monkey**
Flying Star: **1**
Good Day: **Snake**
Bad Day: **Tiger**

08 | AUGUST 2026

The Fire Horse Year

27 Thursday
Animal: **Water Rooster**
Flying Star: **9**
Good Day: **Dragon**
Bad Day: **Rabbit**

28 Friday
Animal: **Water Dog**
Flying Star: **8**
Good Day: **Rabbit**
Bad Day: **Dragon**

29 Saturday
Animal: **Wood Pig**
Flying Star: **7**
Good Day: **Tiger**
Bad Day: **Snake**

30 Sunday
Animal: **Wood Rat**
Flying Star: **6**
Good Day: **Ox**
Bad Day: **Horse**

31 Monday
Animal: **Fire Ox**
Flying Star: **5**
Good Day: **Rat**
Bad Day: **Goat**

1 Tuesday
Animal: **Earth Tiger**
Flying Star: **4**
Good Day: **Pig**
Bad Day: **Monkey**

2 Wednesday
Animal: **Earth Rabbit**
Flying Star: **3**
Good Day: **Dog**
Bad Day: **Rooster**

September 8 – October 7 is the Month of the Rooster

Rooster Chinese Horoscope 2025: Embracing Passion and Transformation

Rooster Birth Years: 1921, 1933, 1945, 1957, 1969, 1981, 1993, 2005, 2017, 2029, 2041

ROOSTER – A Year of Expansion, Activity, and Conscious Growth in the Fire Horse Cycle

2026 promises to be a year of movement, development, and vibrant possibilities for those born under the intelligent and industrious sign of the Rooster. Though you share a clashing relationship with the ruling Yang Fire Horse, the year's energy still carries abundant potential for growth, progress, and exciting new experiences. The Fire Horse encourages you to step into visibility, take decisive action, and bring well-laid plans to life.

This will be a lively, fast-paced year – filled with travel, events, and opportunities that keep you in motion. Yet, it is also a year that tests your adaptability and emotional balance. The key to success lies in maintaining humility, diplomacy, and grace under pressure. By tempering your sharp insight with tact and patience, you can transform the year's challenges into a rewarding and expansive chapter.

Career & Opportunities

Your professional world in 2026 will be buzzing with energy. Projects, collaborations, and opportunities will unfold quickly, sometimes simultaneously. The Fire Horse energy supports advancement, but it also introduces unpredictability – sudden changes in leadership, direction, or workload may arise.

To thrive, Roosters must stay flexible and centred, balancing confidence with cooperation. Your natural precision and organisational skill are assets, but excessive pride or stubbornness can create unnecessary friction. Maintain harmonious relationships with colleagues and superiors by choosing diplomacy over debate.

If you remain open-minded and adaptable, this can be a breakthrough year for visibility and success. Present your ideas with clarity, but also allow others to contribute – teamwork will prove more potent than solo effort.

Tip: Let your excellence speak for itself. Stay humble, focused, and cooperative, and you'll earn recognition naturally.

Wealth & Prosperity

Financially, 2026 presents both promise and caution. The Fire Horse year stimulates prosperity through activity, innovation, and brilliant timing, yet it also encourages risk-taking – something Roosters must approach carefully. Income growth is likely, but so too is the temptation to overspend or stretch finances too thin.

Avoid speculative ventures, impulsive purchases, or investments made on excitement rather than analysis. Property and long-term investments may be favourable if handled with research, prudence, and expert advice. Protect your assets by creating a solid financial plan and adhering to it, even when opportunities seem too good to pass up.

Tip: True wealth this year comes from strategic stability. Grow your finances with patience, and safeguard your resources with foresight.

Love & Relationships

The Rooster, like the Horse, is blessed with Peach Blossom energy in 2026 – an influence that enhances attractiveness, charisma, and social magnetism. Singles will find themselves easily noticed and admired, attracting exciting romantic prospects through travel, work, or social activities.

However, with this charm comes complexity. The same energy that fuels romance can also invite entanglements or unwanted attention. Exercise discernment when meeting new people, and maintain emotional integrity to avoid misunderstandings or scandal.

For those already in relationships, passion is rekindled, but boundaries and loyalty become essential. The Fire Horse's intensity can amplify both love and conflict, so approach communication with patience and tenderness.

Tip: Let love be uplifting, not chaotic. Keep your heart open but your values strong – attraction is powerful, but authenticity sustains it.

Health & Well-being

With such a busy and dynamic year ahead, maintaining physical and emotional balance becomes essential. The Fire Horse's high energy can lead to restlessness, overexertion, or burnout if you don't pace yourself. Schedule downtime, eat nourishing foods, and prioritise regular exercise to ground excess Fire energy.

Mind-body balance practices such as tai chi, stretching, or mindful breathing will help calm your system and support vitality. Pay attention to your cardiovascular and digestive health, especially under stress or when travelling frequently.

Tip: Balance action with rest. Renewing your energy through quiet reflection will keep you strong and radiant throughout the year.

Symbolism of the Rooster and Fire Horse

- The Rooster symbolises precision, confidence, and self-expression – a sign of order, discipline, and keen perception.
- The Fire Horse symbolises momentum, passion, and courage – its energy drives innovation, exploration, and rapid transformation.

Together, they create a year where structure meets spontaneity. When the Rooster's discipline harmonises with the Horse's vitality, significant progress unfolds – but when pride meets impatience, sparks may fly. The lesson is to lead with awareness, communicate with warmth, and stay adaptable amidst the whirlwind of activity.

Final Overview Tip for 2026

This is your year to act boldly yet wisely. The Fire Horse brings motion, visibility, and opportunity, while you get clarity, intelligence, and focus. Stay centred in your purpose, communicate with humility, and channel your energy into meaningful pursuits. By blending courage with caution and charisma with sincerity, you'll emerge from 2026 stronger, wiser, and ready for the next stage of success.

SEPTEMBER Flying Star 1: Triumph, Victory, and Brilliance

September brings forth the luminous double energy of Flying Star 1, a beacon of positivity in the cosmic tapestry. Known as the Star of Triumph, this celestial force radiates its benevolent influence across fame, wealth, intelligence, and success. Its presence ushers in a season ripe for growth, achievement, and brilliance, casting a glow of opportunity over all who fall under its light.

With the guiding hand of Flying Star 1, individuals find themselves on pathways to triumph and victory. Its influence reaches far and wide, from elevating careers and reputations to enhancing status and recognition. This star particularly shines in career advancement and academic excellence, fuelling writing, research, and scholarly pursuits. In this celestial symphony, Flying Star 1 creates a harmonious environment where the seeds of success are sown and nurtured to fruition.

The optimism carried by this star is not fleeting; it lays the foundation for enduring triumphs. Whether overcoming competition, realising long-held dreams, or seizing wealth opportunities, the dynamic energy of Flying Star 1 fosters an atmosphere where influence and success flourish.

In addition to its career-enhancing qualities, Flying Star 1 offers a protective shield against health concerns, bolstering resilience and vitality. However, it also calls for mindfulness in navigating emotional turbulence. Maintaining emotional stability and guarding against depression is essential during this period, as the star's energy can amplify both positive and negative states.

Flying Star 1's elemental essence is Water, and it channels its triumph through this fluid and powerful conduit. Activating its potential involves introducing Yang energy, symbolised by metallic elements such as wind chimes, collections of trophies, or medals that resonate with the star's victorious spirit. Flowing water features, such as fountains or a Victory Horse figurine accompanied by a Ruyi, further align the energies, paving the way for prosperity and success to flow effortlessly into your life.

In 2026, the annual Flying Star 1 will influence the Centre sector of the Luo Shu or Bagua School of Feng Shui. This sector is crucial for nurturing health and well-being, encompassing physical, emotional, and spiritual dimensions.

The centre of your home should remain open and unobstructed to ensure a healthy flow of energy. Any blockages, such as those caused by staircases or bathrooms, can disrupt this flow. To counteract these issues, the area should be infused with the grounding energy of the Earth Element. Employ square shapes, earthy tones like yellow and tan, and ceramic tiles to restore balance and enhance vitality.

Refer to page 12 for this month flying star chart

09 | SEPTEMBER
| 2026

The Fire Horse Year

3
Thursday

Animal: **Metal Dragon**
Flying Star: **2**
Good Day: **Rooster**
Bad Day: **Dog**

4
Friday

Animal: **Metal Snake**
Flying Star: **1**
Good Day: **Monkey**
Bad Day: **Pig**

5
Saturday

Animal: **Water Horse**
Flying Star: **9**
Good Day: **Goat**
Bad Day: **Rat**

6
Sunday

Animal: **Water Goat**
Flying Star: **8**
Good Day: **Horse**
Bad Day: **Ox**

7
Monday

Animal: **Wood Monkey**
Flying Star: **7**
Good Day: **Snake**
Bad Day: **Tiger**

8
Tuesday

Animal: **Wood Rooster**
Flying Star: **6**
Good Day: **Dragon**
Bad Day: **Dog**

9
Wednesday

Animal: **Fire Dog**
Flying Star: **5**
Good Day: **Rabbit**
Bad Day: **Dragon**

SEPTEMBER MONTHLY 2026 CHINESE ZODIAC OVERVIEW

RAT

Steady progress continues, particularly in financial matters. Maintain practical expectations and wise spending habits. For entrepreneurs, this is a period to consolidate rather than expand. Be patient; opportunities will mature in their own time. Stability brings peace.

OX

A busy and fulfilling month that keeps you on your toes. Professionally, advancement and recognition are within reach, particularly if you reimagine your role or presentation. Networking and travel enhance your prospects. Despite the fast pace, this is a rewarding time that fuels motivation and growth.

TIGER

Challenges may test your patience, but your resilience and confidence will set you apart. Even when plans shift, remain calm — flexibility opens doors that rigidity closes. The seeds of opportunity are there; they require time and the proper perspective to bloom.

RABBIT

Energy fluctuates, but overall improvement is on the horizon. At work, patience and thoughtful decision-making will prevent unnecessary stress. Finances show positive movement, and some may enjoy an increase in income or recognition. Relationship energy is harmonious, making this an excellent time to deepen bonds and share appreciation with loved ones.

DRAGON

A potentially stressful month that calls for emotional discipline and self-care. Energy levels may waver, and frustration could arise if expectations are too high. Maintain composure and flexibility to handle challenges effectively. Financially, it's not the best time for major decisions — wait for clearer signals before committing.

SNAKE

Confidence and optimism rise, and your efforts begin to show results. Work and business require focus, but your persistence will pay off. Financial prospects are strong, and some may enjoy a boost in income. Social life blossoms — singles, in particular, may meet meaningful connections through shared interests and social circles.

09 | SEPTEMBER 2026

The Fire Horse Year

10 Thursday
Animal: **Fire Pig**
Flying Star: **4**
Good Day: **Tiger**
Bad Day: **Snake**

11 Friday
Animal: **Earth Rat**
Flying Star: **3**
Good Day: **Ox**
Bad Day: **Horse**

12 Saturday
Animal: **Earth Ox**
Flying Star: **2**
Good Day: **Rat**
Bad Day: **Goat**

13 Sunday
Animal: **Metal Tiger**
Flying Star: **1**
Good Day: **Pig**
Bad Day: **Monkey**

14 Monday
Animal: **Metal Rabbit**
Flying Star: **9**
Good Day: **Dog**
Bad Day: **Rooster**

15 Tuesday
Animal: **Water Dragon**
Flying Star: **8**
Good Day: **Rooster**
Bad Day: **Dog**

16 Wednesday
Animal: **Water Snake**
Flying Star: **7**
Good Day: **Monkey**
Bad Day: **Pig**

HORSE

Energy shifts sharply, creating bursts of intensity and restlessness. Avoid reacting hastily — patience and clear communication will prevent misunderstandings. Short trips, leisure activities, or creative outlets will help balance the stress. Networking and social events prove fruitful, offering valuable connections for future collaborations.

GOAT

Positive energy continues to strengthen your confidence and vitality. Progress accelerates, and opportunities appear through teamwork and cooperation. Keep your focus on long-term outcomes rather than quick wins. If emotional tension surfaces in relationships, remember that kindness and clear communication will always lead back to harmony.

MONKEY

Challenges may test your patience and endurance. Competition at work intensifies, requiring you to stay calm, composed, and tactical. Avoid confrontation by keeping communication direct yet diplomatic. Relationships may experience tension — empathy and compromise are key—schedule time to rest or reflect to maintain focus and inner harmony.

ROOSTER

A joyful and empowering month that reawakens inspiration. Work and creative projects thrive, and leadership opportunities may present themselves. Financial prospects look bright, with profits and gains highlighted. Social engagements bring celebration, and relationships — personal or romantic — flow with ease and connection.

DOG

The pace eases, offering time to pause and reflect. Go with the flow rather than resisting change. Relationships may need extra nurturing, but kindness and patience will dissolve tension. Use this quieter period to recharge your spirit, reorganise priorities, and prepare for the next wave of opportunity.

PIG

Mindfulness and balance are the themes of the month. Work runs smoothly, and supportive people will appear to assist your progress. Travel or short retreats will refresh your perspective. Socially, it's a delightful time to connect — singles may meet someone intriguing, while family and close friends offer warmth and encouragement.

09 | SEPTEMBER 2026

The Fire Horse Year

17 Thursday
Animal: **Wood Horse**
Flying Star: **6**
Good Day: **Goat**
Bad Day: **Rat**

🐎

18 Friday
Animal: **Wood Goat**
Flying Star: **5**
Good Day: **Horse**
Bad Day: **Ox**

⚡

19 Saturday
Animal: **Fire Monkey**
Flying Star: **4**
Good Day: **Snake**
Bad Day: **Tiger**

❤️

20 Sunday
Animal: **Fire Rooster**
Flying Star: **3**
Good Day: **Dragon**
Bad Day: **Dog**

✈️

21 Monday
Animal: **Earth Dog**
Flying Star: **2**
Good Day: **Rabbit**
Bad Day: **Dragon**

👷 🎊 🎉 👓 ✈️

22 Tuesday
Animal: **Earth Pig**
Flying Star: **1**
Good Day: **Tiger**
Bad Day: **Snake**

✏️ 🎉 👓 🏠

23 Wednesday
Animal: **Metal Rat**
Flying Star: **9**
Good Day: **Ox**
Bad Day: **Horse**

CREATING ZODIAC LOVE OPPORTUNITIES

Enhancing Peach Blossom Luck with Feng Shui: For those seeking to enhance their love luck, placing specific animal images in designated areas of your home can activate peach blossom luck, creating opportunities for love and relationships. Here's how you can do it based on your Chinese Animal sign:

For the Snake, Rooster, and Ox: To activate peach blossom luck, place a beautiful horse image in the South of your home, ideally in your bedroom. If the South corner is a toilet or storeroom, set the image in your garden or the South area of your living room. Patience is crucial, as ending unpromising ones may clear the way for a real relationship.

For the Rat, Dragon, and Monkey: Place a rooster image in the West corner of your home or bedroom. The image size is irrelevant, but it should be confident and proud. The gender of the rooster image does not matter; the goal is to activate peach blossom luck, not to attract a rooster partner.

For the Rabbit, Goat, and Pig: Those born under these signs should place a well-made rat figurine, or image, in the North direction of their home or bedroom. This placement activates peach blossom luck.

For the Horse, Dog, and Tiger: Place a rabbit image in the East direction of your home or bedroom. This activation helps create situations conducive to meeting someone with relationship intentions.

By following these Feng Shui guidelines, you can enhance your love luck and create opportunities for meaningful relationships.

However, your partner's quality and the relationship's longevity depend on your destiny and karma.

Key Considerations

- **Quality of Symbols**: Ensure that decorative items used for feng shui are well-made. Place an image or artwork instead if you cannot acquire a decorative item.
- **Realistic Expectations**: Feng shui creates energy conducive to opportunities and possibilities but does not change destiny or control someone's feelings. It accounts for one-third of your luck; the rest depends on your karmic destiny action and choices.

09 | SEPTEMBER 2026

The Fire Horse Year

24 Thursday
Animal: **Metal Ox**
Flying Star: **8**
Good Day: **Rat**
Bad Day: **Goat**

25 Friday
Animal: **Water Tiger**
Flying Star: **7**
Good Day: **Pig**
Bad Day: **Monkey**

26 Saturday
Animal: **Water Rabbit**
Flying Star: **6**
Good Day: **Dog**
Bad Day: **Rooster**

27 Sunday
Animal: **Wood Dragon**
Flying Star: **5**
Good Day: **Rooster**
Bad Day: **Dog**

28 Monday
Animal: **Wood Snake**
Flying Star: **4**
Good Day: **Monkey**
Bad Day: **Pig**

29 Tuesday
Animal: **Fire Horse**
Flying Star: **3**
Good Day: **Goat**
Bad Day: **Rat**

30 Wednesday
Animal: **Fire Goat**
Flying Star: **2**
Good Day: **Horse**
Bad Day: **Ox**

2026 Chinese Astrology Planner

09 SEPTEMBER 2026

The Fire Horse Year

1 Thursday
Animal: **Earth Monkey**
Flying Star: **1**
Good Day: **Snake**
Bad Day: **Tiger**

2 Friday
Animal: **Earth Rooster**
Flying Star: **9**
Good Day: **Dragon**
Bad Day: **Rabbit**

3 Saturday
Animal: **Metal Dog**
Flying Star: **8**
Good Day: **Rabbit**
Bad Day: **Dragon**

4 Sunday
Animal: **Metal Pig**
Flying Star: **7**
Good Day: **Tiger**
Bad Day: **Snake**

5 Monday
Animal: **Water Rat**
Flying Star: **6**
Good Day: **Ox**
Bad Day: **Horse**

6 Tuesday
Animal: **Water Ox**
Flying Star: **5**
Good Day: **Rat**
Bad Day: **Goat**

7 Wednesday
Animal: **Wood Tiger**
Flying Star: **4**
Good Day: **Pig**
Bad Day: **Monkey**

October 8 – November 6 is the Month of the Dog

Dog Chinese Horoscope 2025: Embracing Passion and Transformation

Dog Birth Years: 1922, 1934, 1946, 1958, 1970, 1982, 1994, 2006, 2018, 2030, 2042

DOG – A Year of Connection, Expansion, and Steady Progress in the Fire Horse Cycle

The Yang Fire Horse of 2026 brings a wave of supportive, lively, and uplifting energy for those born under the loyal and grounded Dog sign. This is a harmonious year where your natural integrity and reliability align beautifully with the Horse's enthusiasm and forward motion. You'll feel more "in rhythm" with life's tempo — opportunities will arise, networks will expand, and your confidence will grow.

That said, not everything moves in a straight line. Pauses or delays will follow moments of acceleration, but these fluctuations are meant to refine your patience and perspective. The key for Dogs this year is to stay adaptable and centered — to meet both movement and stillness with grace. When you flow with timing rather than resist it, the year unfolds with steady, meaningful progress.

Career & Opportunities

The Fire Horse year energises your professional life, encouraging learning, growth, and renewed motivation. You may feel inspired to expand your skills, study new subjects, or explore unfamiliar industries. These self-development efforts are highly favoured — short courses, online certifications, and workshops can lead to valuable insights and even new career directions.

Those in leadership or mentoring roles will find fulfilment in sharing knowledge, while others may benefit from guidance and training. The Dog's dependable nature attracts trust, and your commitment to quality work will not go unnoticed. Travel, conferences, and networking events are also highlighted — each offering potential for professional expansion and collaboration.

Tip: Approach progress as a journey, not a race. The more you invest in learning and genuine relationships, the greater your long-term rewards.

Wealth & Prosperity

Financially, 2026 holds stability with potential for modest gains. The Fire Horse's influence brings activity and momentum, but also fluctuating expenses — particularly related to travel, education, or social events. To stay balanced, focus on practical money management and avoid impulsive spending during periods of enthusiasm or stress.

Investments in self-improvement or professional growth will prove more beneficial than speculative ventures. If you remain patient and prudent, you'll lay the groundwork for a more prosperous future cycle.

Tip: Build wealth through knowledge and discipline. Sustainable success grows from informed choices, not fleeting trends.

Love & Relationships

Socially, this is one of your more engaging years. The Fire Horse stirs up a lively atmosphere, bringing celebrations, community events, and joyful gatherings. Friendships blossom, and new connections enter your circle – some of which may become long-lasting or influential.

For singles, romance may spark in social or group settings, particularly through travel, shared interests, or learning environments. Be open to meeting people from different walks of life. For those already in relationships, warmth, understanding, and companionship deepen, provided you maintain healthy communication and balance shared time with personal space.

Tip: Let connection flow naturally. Relationships – romantic or otherwise – thrive when you lead with sincerity and humor rather than expectation.

Health & Well-being

With a full schedule and increased social activity, self-care becomes essential. The Fire Horse energy can heighten busyness, leading to fatigue if rest is neglected. Prioritise balance and recovery through moderate exercise, grounding routines, and time in nature.

Spa retreats, yoga, or meditation will help you reset your energy, while simple pleasures like time with loved ones or pets will restore emotional calm. Pay attention to your digestive and nervous systems – both are sensitive to stress this year.

Tip: Pace yourself. You don't have to attend every event or say yes to every invitation. Rest is as valuable as action.

Symbolism of the Dog and Fire Horse

- The Dog symbolises loyalty, wisdom, and integrity – the guardian of truth, friendship, and justice.
- The Fire Horse symbolises vitality, courage, and enthusiasm – the force that propels change and reinvention.

Together, they form a partnership of faithful fire – where reliability meets passion, and movement aligns with purpose. The Dog's loyalty balances the Horse's intensity, creating a year of grounded enthusiasm and meaningful growth.

Final Overview Tip for 2026

This is a year to reconnect – with others, with your goals, and with yourself. The Fire Horse opens doors for learning, travel, and joyful expansion, but it also reminds you to honour your limits and rest when needed. By pacing your energy, nurturing genuine relationships, and embracing curiosity, you'll find that 2026 becomes a year of renewal, fulfilment, and quiet achievement.

OCTOBER Flying Star 9: Abundant Prosperity and Beyond

October rejoices under the luminous influence of Flying Star 9, a radiant beacon in the celestial tapestry. Known as the Star of Current Prosperity, this star shines brilliantly over completion, fame, celebration, wealth, intelligence, popularity, happiness, and acclaim. As a dynamic Fire Star, its vibrant energy sparks a cascade of joyous gatherings and festive occasions, inviting all to bask in its auspicious glow. Dubbed the "Star of Completion," Flying Star 9 brings projects and endeavours to their triumphant conclusion, nurturing financial success and prosperity. This is a special monthly combination with yearly flying star 1 combining with flying star 9 to form a lucky sum of ten luck.

This star is a powerful catalyst for both present and future ventures, magnifying the means of abundance and ensuring that the seeds of effort previously sown bear fruit. Its influence is particularly potent, as Flying Star 9 illuminates their paths with its brilliant energy. Those aligned with this star, especially the eldest daughter and those born under the Dragon and Snake zodiacs, are encouraged to embrace challenges enthusiastically, knowing victory is within reach.

As the ultimate harbinger of prosperity, Flying Star 9 accelerates wealth accumulation, boosts business profits, and enhances investments. It also elevates fame and recognition, casting a celestial spotlight on those pursuing success in various fields. In the current cosmic configuration, Flying Star 9 is the most potent force among the divine energies, making engaging with spaces influenced by it highly beneficial. Whether embarking on new business ventures, planning a wedding, or starting a family, the energy of Flying Star 9 offers a powerful boost to these life-changing endeavours.

To amplify its auspicious energy, incorporate wealth-enhancing symbols into your surroundings. Consider placing a wealth jar, a trio of horses, or Buddha figurines in prominent positions. Arranging 9 Gold Coins on a tassel or displaying a Wealth God figure and Gold Ingots further strengthens the star's influence. Multiples of nine, vibrant lighting, and red-themed decor—such as red phoenix symbols, upholstery, and accessories—elevate the energy even more. For an extra touch of prosperity, introduce a water feature with nine fish to amplify the flow of abundance.

Flying Star 9 emerges as a radiant symbol of prosperity and joy, guiding all who embrace its effervescent energy toward a bountiful journey ahead.

In 2026, the annual Flying Star 9 will influence the Southeast sector of the Luo Shu (Bagua) School of Feng Shui. Traditionally associated with wealth, prosperity, and financial growth, this sector offers fertile ground for enhancing income, cash flow, and overall economic success. It brings optimism and potential for monetary advancement, making it an area ripe for strategic Feng Shui adjustments.

The Southeast is governed by the Wood element, which thrives on the nurturing qualities of Water. To amplify the financial opportunities symbolised by Flying Star 9, enhance this sector with water-themed elements such as a water feature or a picturesque water image. Water strengthens the Wood energy and harmonises with green hues, plants, and floral decorations, further supporting financial luck. Ensure that the water flow is directed inward, enhancing the flow of prosperity into your home rather than allowing it to exit.

Refer to page 12 for this month flying star chart

10 | OCTOBER 2026

The Fire Horse Year

8
Thursday

Animal: **Wood Rabbit**
Flying Star: **3**
Good Day: **Dog**
Bad Day: **Dragon**

9
Friday

Animal: **Fire Dragon**
Flying Star: **2**
Good Day: **Rooster**
Bad Day: **Dog**

10
Saturday

Animal: **Fire Snake**
Flying Star: **1**
Good Day: **Monkey**
Bad Day: **Pig**

11
Sunday

Animal: **Earth Horse**
Flying Star: **9**
Good Day: **Goat**
Bad Day: **Rat**

12
Monday

Animal: **Earth Goat**
Flying Star: **8**
Good Day: **Horse**
Bad Day: **Ox**

13
Tuesday

Animal: **Metal Monkey**
Flying Star: **7**
Good Day: **Snake**
Bad Day: **Tiger**

14
Wednesday

Animal: **Metal Rooster**
Flying Star: **6**
Good Day: **Dragon**
Bad Day: **Rabbit**

2026 Chinese Astrology Planner

OCTOBER MONTHLY 2026 CHINESE ZODIAC OVERVIEW

RAT

Dynamic energy propels you forward. Projects speed up, connections strengthen, and your ideas gain traction. This is an excellent period to expand your network, meet new allies, or reconnect with valuable contacts. Relationships – personal and professional – blossom beautifully under this influence.

OX

A gentler rhythm returns, allowing you to breathe and regroup. Use this month to tidy up loose ends and finalise pending matters. Mid-month, stay alert to shifting circumstances – discernment is key before saying yes to sudden offers. Calm observation and wise timing bring better outcomes than haste.

TIGER

Energy dips, and you may feel mentally or emotionally drained. Slow your pace and allow yourself time to recharge. Avoid overcommitting – rest is productive, too. Mindful communication helps to ease tension and deepen your relationships. Observation and stillness bring clarity.

RABBIT

An outstanding month for Rabbits. Your talents and reliability shine, drawing admiration and new opportunities. It's a time to step forward with confidence and showcase your strengths. Financial luck is steady but calls for cautious planning – avoid speculation and focus on sustainable, long-term rewards.

DRAGON

Shifting energy tests your determination and adaptability. Progress may feel uneven, but new opportunities can emerge through persistence. Manage your schedule carefully and prioritise tasks – burnout is possible if you try to do too much. Keep perspective; patience now creates stability later.

SNAKE

Energy fluctuates more dramatically this month, bringing twists before things settle. Plans may shift direction, so patience and strategy are vital. Avoid impulsive moves in finances or relationships. Steady, thoughtful action ensures sustainable success, while open communication maintains personal harmony.

HORSE

A dynamic and fast-moving month filled with opportunities and challenges. Business and work matters accelerate, but avoid overcommitting. Review details carefully to prevent miscommunication or paperwork errors. Networking remains a lucky pursuit,

10 | OCTOBER 2026

The Fire Horse Year

15 Thursday
Animal: **Water Dog**
Flying Star: **5**
Good Day: **Rabbit**
Bad Day: **Dragon**

⚡ ✈️ 🏠

16 Friday
Animal: **Water Pig**
Flying Star: **4**
Good Day: **Tiger**
Bad Day: **Snake**

💅 ✈️ ❤️

17 Saturday
Animal: **Wood Rat**
Flying Star: **3**
Good Day: **Ox**
Bad Day: **Horse**

💅 💍

18 Sunday
Animal: **Wood Ox**
Flying Star: **2**
Good Day: **Rat**
Bad Day: **Goat**

🧑‍🦳

19 Monday
Animal: **Fire Tiger**
Flying Star: **1**
Good Day: **Pig**
Bad Day: **Monkey**

🗳️

20 Tuesday
Animal: **Fire Rabbit**
Flying Star: **9**
Good Day: **Dog**
Bad Day: **Dragon**

🗳️ ✈️

21 Wednesday
Animal: **Earth Dragon**
Flying Star: **8**
Good Day: **Rooster**
Bad Day: **Dog**

yielding beneficial alliances and potential partnerships—balance activity with rest to sustain momentum.

GOAT

A competitive energy comes into play, especially in professional settings. Avoid getting drawn into unnecessary disputes or rivalries – neutrality and tact will serve you best. Finances remain steady, but this is not the time for indulgent spending. Socially, singles will enjoy a lively and engaging month filled with connections and shared joy.

MONKEY

Constructive and productive energy flows in, creating opportunities for advancement. This is a favourable month to take decisive steps toward your goals. Financial prospects improve, particularly through thoughtful planning or negotiation. Relationships strengthen through kindness and shared experiences – progress feels tangible and satisfying.

ROOSTER

Uncertainty may linger early in the month, encouraging reflection and refinement. New partnerships or collaborations should be approached with discernment – do your research before committing. As the month unfolds, energy turns increasingly positive, allowing progress and renewed focus on your business or career goals.

DOG

A constructive month that rewards steady effort and optimism. Flexibility in thought and approach will open doors to success at work. Financially, energy is moderate – practical spending and wise budgeting are recommended. Invest in your health through fresh air, movement, and activities that lift your spirit. Progress now comes from consistency rather than haste.

PIG

Energy fluctuates slightly, reminding you to slow down and reassess priorities. Use this time to consolidate efforts, review projects, and ensure everything is aligned for long-term stability. Practising self-care through nature walks, creative outlets, or gentle movement will help maintain emotional calm and physical vitality.

10 OCTOBER 2026

The Fire Horse Year

22 Thursday
Animal: **Earth Snake**
Flying Star: **7**
Good Day: **Monkey**
Bad Day: **Pig**

23 Friday
Animal: **Metal Horse**
Flying Star: **6**
Good Day: **Goat**
Bad Day: **Rat**

24 Saturday
Animal: **Metal Goat**
Flying Star: **5**
Good Day: **Horse**
Bad Day: **Ox**

25 Sunday
Animal: **Water Monkey**
Flying Star: **4**
Good Day: **Snake**
Bad Day: **Tiger**

26 Monday
Animal: **Water Rooster**
Flying Star: **3**
Good Day: **Dragon**
Bad Day: **Rabbit**

27 Tuesday
Animal: **Wood Dog**
Flying Star: **2**
Good Day: **Rabbit**
Bad Day: **Dragon**

28 Wednesday
Animal: **Wood Pig**
Flying Star: **1**
Good Day: **Tiger**
Bad Day: **Snake**

10

OCTOBER
2026

The Fire Horse Year

29 Thursday
Animal: **Fire Rat**
Flying Star: **9**
Good Day: **Ox**
Bad Day: **Horse**

30 Friday
Animal: **Fire Ox**
Flying Star: **8**
Good Day: **Rat**
Bad Day: **Goat**

31 Saturday
Animal: **Earth Tiger**
Flying Star: **7**
Good Day: **Pig**
Bad Day: **Monkey**

1 Sunday
Animal: **Earth Rabbit**
Flying Star: **6**
Good Day: **Dog**
Bad Day: **Rooster**

2 Monday
Animal: **Metal Dragon**
Flying Star: **5**
Good Day: **Rooster**
Bad Day: **Dog**

3 Tuesday
Animal: **Metal Snake**
Flying Star: **4**
Good Day: **Monkey**
Bad Day: **Pig**

4 Wednesday
Animal: **Water Horse**
Flying Star: **3**
Good Day: **Goat**
Bad Day: **Rat**

November 7 - December 6 is the Month of the Pig

Pig Chinese Horoscope 2025: Embracing Change and Transformation

Pig Birth Years: 1923, 1935, 1947, 1959, 1971, 1983, 1995, 2007, 2019, 2031, 2043

PIG – A Year of Renewal, Opportunity, and Inspired Growth in the Fire Horse Cycle

The Yang Fire Horse of 2026 arrives with light, optimism, and forward momentum, ushering in a period of renewal and upward movement for those born under the gentle and compassionate Pig sign. After several years of fluctuation, this is a refreshing and empowering phase that restores enthusiasm, confidence, and direction.

You will feel more energised, motivated, and optimistic, with auspicious stars shining upon your sign, illuminating your natural warmth, generosity, and wisdom. These supportive influences enhance your strengths – attracting helpful people, inspiring new ideas, and opening doors to both personal and professional advancement. The key to thriving this year is to balance enthusiasm with discernment and to take bold yet thoughtful steps toward your goals.

Career & Opportunities

In your professional world, 2026 signals movement, recognition, and new beginnings. The Fire Horse energy brings vitality and opportunity – whether through a change in role, business expansion, or a fresh career direction altogether.

For some Pigs, this may be the year to embrace a complete reinvention, stepping into new fields aligned with passion and purpose. For others, the rewards will come from refining existing skills and expanding what you've already built. Those engaged in academia, research, or self-development will find their efforts rewarded, as focus and perseverance lead to visible achievement.

This is also an auspicious time to network, collaborate, or launch creative ventures, as your charisma and communication skills attract support and positive attention.

Tip: Say yes to new horizons – but move with mindfulness. Thoughtful planning ensures your progress remains steady and sustainable.

Wealth & Prosperity

Financially, this is a year of promise and growth, but it comes with a reminder to balance optimism with caution. The Fire Horse favours entrepreneurial ventures, creative projects, and innovative partnerships – areas where your sincerity and intuition can shine. Sudden opportunities may appear, offering unexpected gains, but hasty decisions or emotional spending could offset progress.

If investing or entering new agreements, perform careful research and seek trusted advice, especially in property, contracts, or significant financial commitments. Your income potential is strong, and with practical management, you can achieve both stability and expansion.

Tip: Let your financial decisions be guided by wisdom, not excitement. Secure your foundations before you gallop ahead.

Love & Relationships

The social and romantic landscape glows brightly for the Pig in 2026. The Fire Horse brings warmth, charisma, and a lively social atmosphere – perfect for meeting new people and deepening existing relationships.

For singles, this is a year of vibrant social connection, filled with exciting encounters and genuine chemistry. Romance may arise through travel, events, or professional networking. For those in committed relationships, harmony is favoured, though mutual understanding is key to maintaining balance amid busy schedules.

As your personal goals expand, remember to nurture emotional closeness. Shared adventures, open communication, and laughter will strengthen the bonds of love and friendship.

Tip: Keep your heart open but your priorities aligned. Joy and stability coexist beautifully when nurtured with presence and intention.

Health & Well-being

The Fire Horse year is lively and active, and for the Pig, this increased pace demands balance and self-care. While your vitality is strong, overcommitment or neglecting rest could lead to fatigue. A consistent routine that includes light exercise, balanced nutrition, and adequate downtime will keep your energy steady.

The digestive system and circulation may require extra attention—eat mindfully, hydrate well, and avoid overindulging in rich foods or late nights. Incorporating mindful practices such as meditation, breathing exercises, or nature walks will help you maintain emotional calm and clarity.

Tip: Pace yourself. Protect your peace as diligently as you pursue your goals, and your inner radiance will shine all year long.

Symbolism of the Pig and Fire Horse

- The Pig symbolises kindness, abundance, and sincerity – it embodies empathy, loyalty, and an appreciation for life's pleasures.
- The Fire Horse symbolises passion, freedom, and drive – it represents motion, courage, and visionary action.

Together, these energies weave a year of compassionate ambition and joyful expansion. The Pig's grounded generosity harmonises with the Horse's fiery vitality, creating the perfect balance between heartfelt living and inspired doing.

Final Overview Tip for 2026

This is a year to embrace renewal and ride the wave of optimism. The Fire Horse infuses your life with enthusiasm and fresh perspective, while auspicious stars light your path with opportunity and support. Stay true to your values, move forward with confidence, and maintain balance between work, play, and rest. When heart and action align, 2026 becomes a year of joyful achievement, emotional fulfilment, and inspired new beginnings.

November, Flying Star 8: Unveiling Abundant Prosperity

November ushers in a steady wave of prosperity with the presence of the retiring Flying Star 8. Within the grand celestial orchestra, this star shines brilliantly as the Star of Prosperity, casting an encompassing glow of wealth, well-being, luxury, renown, financial prowess, and lasting success. Flying Star 8 is a beacon of affluence, bringing monetary fortune, nobility, and enduring stability. Under its benevolent light, one can anticipate increased income, financial triumphs, and the fortunate alignment of power and influence. As its radiant energy resonates, professional pursuits flourish, enhancing reputation and recognition for hard work. To align with this favourable tide is to unlock a world of growing potential.

For homes with an East-facing main door or a living or family area in this sector, Flying Star 8's optimistic energy becomes an all-encompassing blessing, especially for the eldest son and those born under the Rabbit sign.

Maintaining a clutter-free space in this sector ensures a smooth energy flow. To activate and amplify its auspicious vibrations, incorporating wealth-related symbols serves as a powerful enhancer. These symbols might include a Buddha figurine, a tassel adorned with 6 Gold Coins, a Wealth God figure, or Gold Ingots. Additionally, strategically placing bright lights, clocks, and televisions, and fostering a bustling environment, significantly boost the star's positive influence. Notably, movement—whether through footsteps or other dynamic actions—remains the most potent conductor of energy in this space.

Flying Star 8's brilliance unveils a realm of luxury and affluence. To embrace its blessings is to enter a world of enduring prosperity and unyielding success.

In 2026, the East sector of the Luo Shu or Bagua School of Feng Shui will be graced by the annual Flying Star 8. This sector, deeply associated with health, longevity, and overall well-being, provides a prime opportunity to enhance these vital aspects of life.

The Wood element governs the East, and incorporating both Wood and Water elements can amplify its positive influence on health and vitality. One practical remedy is to place bamboo in a water feature, as this combination strengthens the Wood element and supports a flourishing state of health. Introducing greenery, plants, and vibrant flowers will further invigorate this sector. The East is also home to the celestial Green Dragon, a symbol of auspicious fortune. Positioning a dragon figurine in this area can optimise the family's luck and overall well-being. Consider placing a Quan Yin statue to safeguard and nurture your physical and emotional vitality, enhancing your protection and health.

Refer to page 12 for this month flying star chart

11 | NOVEMBER 2026

The Fire Horse Year

5
Thursday

Animal: **Water Goat**
Flying Star: **2**
Good Day: **Horse**
Bad Day: **Ox**

6
Friday

Animal: **Wood Monkey**
Flying Star: **1**
Good Day: **Snake**
Bad Day: **Tiger**

7
Saturday

Animal: **Wood Rooster**
Flying Star: **9**
Good Day: **Dragon**
Bad Day: **Rabbit**

8
Sunday

Animal: **Fire Dog**
Flying Star: **8**
Good Day: **Rabbit**
Bad Day: **Dragon**

9
Monday

Animal: **Fire Pig**
Flying Star: **7**
Good Day: **Tiger**
Bad Day: **Snake**

10
Tuesday

Animal: **Earth Rat**
Flying Star: **6**
Good Day: **Ox**
Bad Day: **Horse**

11
Wednesday

Animal: **Earth Ox**
Flying Star: **5**
Good Day: **Rat**
Bad Day: **Goat**

2026 Chinese Astrology Planner

NOVEMBER MONTHLY 2026 CHINESE ZODIAC OVERVIEW

RAT

Your stamina may dip temporarily, reminding you to slow down and recharge. Delegate where possible, and don't push beyond your limits. Accept support graciously. A short retreat, time in nature, or simply disconnecting from noise will help realign your focus and vitality.

OX

Energy accelerates once again, pushing you into action. Stay focused and manage your schedule with structure to prevent overwhelm. Financial support is strong, and your hard work begins to show results. Recharge through outdoor exercise or grounding activities – balance is essential to maintain peak performance.

TIGER

A smoother flow of energy lifts your spirits. Business and career matters are progressing, and financial prospects are improving. This is also an excellent time for travel, leisure, and self-renewal. Relationships enjoy harmony and growth, bringing warmth and connection back into your world.

RABBIT

A bustling, fast-paced month filled with activity. Time management becomes crucial as professional and personal demands increase. Financially, stability continues, and with wise planning, you can build lasting security. Stay strategic rather than reactive – careful choices now will yield steady gains later.

DRAGON

Optimism and renewed motivation return, revitalising your outlook. Business and professional matters expand, and networking brings promising connections– financial energy steadies, supporting practical investments or savings plans. Personal relationships may still require an understanding, empathetic, and balanced approach.

SNAKE

Transformative energy arrives, nudging you to reassess priorities. This may initially feel disruptive, but ultimately clears the way for better alignment. Flexibility and cooperation will ease workplace challenges. Loved ones may need extra time and attention – balance your responsibilities and nurture harmony in your personal world.

11

NOVEMBER 2026

The Fire Horse Year

12
Thursday

Animal: **Metal Tiger**
Flying Star: **4**
Good Day: **Pig**
Bad Day: **Monkey**

13
Friday

Animal: **Metal Rabbit**
Flying Star: **3**
Good Day: **Dog**
Bad Day: **Rooster**

14
Saturday

Animal: **Water Dragon**
Flying Star: **2**
Good Day: **Rooster**
Bad Day: **Dog**

15
Sunday

Animal: **Water Snake**
Flying Star: **1**
Good Day: **Monkey**
Bad Day: **Pig**

16
Monday

Animal: **Wood Horse**
Flying Star: **9**
Good Day: **Goat**
Bad Day: **Rat**

17
Tuesday

Animal: **Wood Goat**
Flying Star: **8**
Good Day: **Horse**
Bad Day: **Ox**

18
Wednesday

Animal: **Fire Monkey**
Flying Star: **7**
Good Day: **Snake**
Bad Day: **Tiger**

HORSE

Workload may increase and demands feel heavier, yet this is a highly productive and financially rewarding month. Gains and new income streams are highlighted – wealth can arrive in unexpected ways. Stay focused, organised, and open-minded. Success comes through consistency, teamwork, and maintaining calm under pressure.

GOAT

Momentum builds beautifully, and projects nurtured throughout the year reach a rewarding stage of completion. Recognition and progress are likely to bring a renewed sense of achievement. Finances stay healthy, but festive gatherings may tempt you to overspend – moderation will keep the balance intact. Gratitude and generosity attract even greater blessings.

MONKEY

A harmonious and fulfilling month arrives, filled with connection and success. Finances look promising, and efforts made earlier in the year begin to pay off. Social energy is vibrant – networking, travel, and community involvement bring beneficial encounters. Relationships blossom, both personally and professionally, under this warm and supportive energy.

ROOSTER

Energy fluctuates slightly, making it an ideal time to consolidate projects and ensure your plans remain on track. Financial stability continues, but speculative risks are best avoided. A busy social schedule may feel overwhelming at times, so prioritise quality connections. Relationships will benefit from presence, patience, and heartfelt communication.

DOG

Harmony returns, and this month favours teamwork and collaboration. Supportive allies and mentors may appear, guiding you toward new opportunities. Career advancement and partnerships are well-established. Socially, the energy sparkles with enjoyable connections. Your health and motivation also improve, making it easier to sustain positive habits.

PIG

A potent and auspicious month filled with success energy. Confidence runs high, and your positivity attracts opportunities. Work and business ventures expand, and past efforts begin to bear fruit. Financially, rewards or recognition are likely. Stay humble, generous, and grateful – your good energy will multiply through kindness.

11 | NOVEMBER 2026

The Fire Horse Year

19 Thursday
Animal: **Fire Rooster**
Flying Star: **6**
Good Day: **Dragon**
Bad Day: **Rabbit**

20 Friday
Animal: **Earth Dog**
Flying Star: **5**
Good Day: **Rabbit**
Bad Day: **Dragon**

21 Saturday
Animal: **Earth Pig**
Flying Star: **4**
Good Day: **Tiger**
Bad Day: **Snake**

22 Sunday
Animal: **Metal Rat**
Flying Star: **3**
Good Day: **Ox**
Bad Day: **Horse**

23 Monday
Animal: **Metal Ox**
Flying Star: **2**
Good Day: **Rat**
Bad Day: **Goat**

24 Tuesday
Animal: **Water Tiger**
Flying Star: **1**
Good Day: **Pig**
Bad Day: **Monkey**

25 Wednesday
Animal: **Water Rabbit**
Flying Star: **9**
Good Day: **Dog**
Bad Day: **Rooster**

11 | NOVEMBER 2026

The Fire Horse Year

26 Thursday
- Animal: **Wood Dragon**
- Flying Star: **8**
- Good Day: **Rooster**
- Bad Day: **Dog**

27 Friday
- Animal: **Wood Snake**
- Flying Star: **7**
- Good Day: **Monkey**
- Bad Day: **Pig**

28 Saturday
- Animal: **Fire Horse**
- Flying Star: **6**
- Good Day: **Goat**
- Bad Day: **Rat**

29 Sunday
- Animal: **Fire Goat**
- Flying Star: **5**
- Good Day: **Horse**
- Bad Day: **Ox**

30 Monday
- Animal: **Earth Monkey**
- Flying Star: **4**
- Good Day: **Snake**
- Bad Day: **Tiger**

1 Tuesday
- Animal: **Earth Rooster**
- Flying Star: **3**
- Good Day: **Dragon**
- Bad Day: **Rabbit**

2 Wednesday
- Animal: **Metal Dog**
- Flying Star: **2**
- Good Day: **Rabbit**
- Bad Day: **Dragon**

December 7, 2024 - January 5, 2025: Month of the Rat

Rat Chinese Horoscope 2025: Embrace Change and Transformation

(1924, 1936, 1948, 1960, 1972, 1984, 1996, 2008, 2020)

Rat – Your Year in the Fire-Horse Cycle

Being the first sign of the Chinese zodiac, the Rat brings a strong foundation of resourcefulness, intelligence and adaptability into this year. And yet, with the year dominated by the Fire Horse energy, the terrain shifts beneath your feet: fast, fiery, unpredictable. The Fire Horse year is not one of quiet consolidation – it urges movement, boldness and change. For you, this means parts of the year will feel exciting and full of potential – and other parts will test you.

Career & Opportunities

In this Fire Horse year, you may find that your usual steady, methodical pace needs to be picked up a notch. Predictions suggest that for Rats, this year is like the "first year of harvest" – a time when earlier efforts begin to bear fruit, but also when you're expected to step forward, act, and seize opportunities.

You may be offered a promotion, a new role, or a project that requires you to act outside your comfort zone. However, the Fire Horse energy favours boldness but also carries risk – for you, the smart move is to plan strategically rather than rush in impulsively.

Your skills, adaptability and mental agility (typical Rat strengths) will serve you well. Still, you'll need to combine them with a readiness to pivot, to upgrade your abilities, and to embrace change rather than resisting it.

Tip: Identify one new skill or platform this year and invest in it – your responsiveness to change can become your golden opportunity.

Wealth & Prosperity

Financially, the year presents both promise and caution. On the one hand, because of the groundwork you've laid, you may see more opportunities for income, bonuses, or streams you set up earlier. The harvest metaphor holds: you've planted, now you may reap.

On the other hand, the Fire Horse influence warns of impulsive spending, speculative investments or over-leverage. Sources urge Rats to manage finances with care, avoid risk-taking, and guard resources rather than assume they'll naturally expand.

So for wealth: you are in a "make or steadying" year – you **can** do well if you treat money like a tool needing discipline. Watch your cash flow, build reserves, and don't chase every shiny opportunity without due diligence.

Tip: Set a realistic budget for the year, earmark a portion of gains for long-term savings, and resist the urge to blow windfalls recklessly.

Love & Relationships

For the Rat, love and relationships this year carry an interesting duality. Your sign naturally has a "Peach Blossom" influence (attractiveness in love) for many years, and some sources suggest this remains in play for you.

However, the Fire Horse year can bring turbulence. While your attractiveness and social circle may expand (you'll meet new people, go to events, connect), the flip side is that existing relationships can feel stressed, miscommunicated, or drift. Indeed, when your sign is "clashing" with the Horse's energy, relationships may be more dynamic or testing.

If you're single: This is a year where meeting someone new is more likely, but depth over flirtation is advisable.

If you're in a committed relationship: You'll need to be disciplined – communicate clearly, avoid hidden resentments, and don't assume things will stay static.

Tip: Choose sincerity over charm. When you feel drawn to someone new, ask: "Could this lead to something stable?" And if you're committed, schedule time for honest check-ins.

Health & Well-Being

The Fire Horse year brings heightened energy, momentum, and possibility – but also the risk of burnout, stress and erratic rhythms. For the Rat, whose natural tendency is to hustle, strategise and keep busy, caution is required: you might push too hard, ignore rest, and skip self-care. Sources suggest that emotional strain, fatigue, and digestive issues may surface if you don't pace yourself.

Thus, your well-being strategy should emphasise grounding, pauses, and mindfulness. Incorporate regular rest, healthy eating, and reflection time to temper the Fire Horse's rush.

Tip: Build a weekly "slow zone" into your routine – no work, no screens, just reading, strolling, breathing. That pause will keep you in good shape.

Symbolism of the Rat + Fire Horse Influence

- The Rat is the first of the zodiac, symbolising beginnings, fresh energy, adaptability and clever survival.
- The Fire Horse adds the themes of passion, independence, rapid movement, courage, restlessness – it amplifies the pace, the boldness, the shine. Chinese Astrology Year+1

So combined: this year is about harnessing your clever, adaptable Rat nature and channelling it into the dynamic, expansive Fire Horse energy – rather than fighting it. You'll be asked to move boldly, but also intelligently; act swiftly, but with strategy; embrace chance, but guard your foundations.

Final Overview Tip for the Year

For Rats, this year is "the harvest begins" – you have what you need, now it's time to step up, **but with care. If you** balance your natural wit with grounded action, adapt with discipline rather than impulse, you'll ride the Fire Horse rather than be bucked off. Make deliberate moves, protect what you've built, and let your energy flow with purpose.

DECEMBER, Flying Star 7: A Multitude of Discord and Unrest

December heralds a period of unrest with the arrival of the ominous Flying Star 7. In the intricate cosmic dance, this inauspicious star ushers in a cacophony of conflict, disputes, legal entanglements, ailments, mishaps, theft, and the unsettling echoes of gossip. The shadow cast by Flying Star 7 is profoundly feared, as it has the potential to sow seeds of rivalry, trespass, theft, and even violence into the fabric of life. During this phase, caution is essential, as one must navigate its treacherous currents with care.

The unsettling energies of this star are particularly potent in matters of emotional and physical well-being, making vigilance crucial for the matriarchs, mothers, older women, or those born under the Goat or Monkey zodiac sign. In professional environments, office politics swell, and rivalries intensify. Trust must be earned as deception and schemes lurk beneath the surface. The Southwest sector, in particular, resonates with this turbulence, and therefore, heightened awareness and vigilance are vital to maintaining tranquillity.

Flying Star 7 also increases the risk of ailments affecting the mouth and teeth, potentially requiring hospitalisation or surgical interventions for those with pre-existing health issues. Traditional remedies become essential in mitigating its disruptive influence. One such remedy involves placing three pieces of bamboo in a clear glass vase filled with water in the Western sector. The symbolic talisman of the Evil Eye, flanked by seven glass elephants, serves as a powerful countermeasure. Positioning a Blue Rhinoceros and a Blue Elephant can protect against this evil energy. As a final safeguard, incorporating a water feature helps to neutralise the metallic energy dominating this space, ensuring the tranquillity and vitality of the surrounding environment.

Flying Star 7's arrival necessitates a mindful approach, as its discordant energies require careful navigation to avoid being swept into its currents of unrest and discord.

In 2026, the Southwest sector of the Luo Shu or Bagua School of Feng Shui will host the annual Flying Star 7. This sector is pivotal for fostering relationship luck, love, romance, and marriage, making it a vital area for enhancing these aspects of life.

The Southwest is associated with the Earth element, and to amplify its positive effects on relationships, integrating both Earth and Fire energies is critical. Enhance this sector with amethyst or rose quartz crystals, and consider incorporating vibrant hues such as purple, pink, and red peonies to support romantic endeavours. The double happiness symbol and a pair of Mandarin Ducks are traditional symbols that signify love and partnership, making them ideal for this area. To further boost the energy, add bright lighting to the Southwest sector to illuminate it with positive, nurturing vibrations.

Refer to page 12 for this month flying star chart

12

DECEMBER
2026

The Fire Horse Year

3 Thursday
Animal: **Metal Pig**
Flying Star: **1**
Good Day: **Tiger**
Bad Day: **Snake**
✈

4 Friday
Animal: **Water Rat**
Flying Star: **9**
Good Day: **Ox**
Bad Day: **Horse**

5 Saturday
Animal: **Water Ox**
Flying Star: **8**
Good Day: **Rat**
Bad Day: **Goat**

6 Sunday
Animal: **Wood Tiger**
Flying Star: **7**
Good Day: **Pig**
Bad Day: **Monkey**

7 Monday
Animal: **Wood Rabbit**
Flying Star: **6**
Good Day: **Dog**
Bad Day: **Rooster**

8 Tuesday
Animal: **Fire Dragon**
Flying Star: **5**
Good Day: **Rooster**
Bad Day: **Dog**

9 Wednesday
Animal: **Fire Snake**
Flying Star: **4**
Good Day: **Monkey**
Bad Day: **Pig**

2026 Chinese Astrology Planner

DECEMBER MONTHLY 2026 CHINESE ZODIAC OVERVIEW

RAT

One of the more intense months, as conflicting energies may create unpredictability. Avoid rushing into commitments or travelling without preparation. Stay flexible and mindful. Gentle exercise, meditation, and grounding rituals will help you maintain calm through fluctuating circumstances.

OX

Vibrant yet demanding, this month may stretch your limits if you don't pace yourself. Work may intensify, and travel plans could increase activity levels. Energy levels fluctuate, so honour your body's needs and prioritise rest when possible. A balanced lifestyle sustains your inner fire through this dynamic period.

TIGER

Events accelerate once more, reigniting creativity and initiative. This is your moment to take the lead and showcase your talents. Financially, stability supports you, though balance remains essential – avoid exhaustion by pacing yourself. Loved ones may need extra attention; kindness and patience will strengthen emotional bonds.

RABBIT

Although energy feels slower and productivity may dip, maintaining consistency will keep you on track. Progress may not be dramatic, but your steady focus lays the foundation for future success. In love, nurture connection through empathy and communication – small gestures strengthen lasting bonds.

DRAGON

A calm, progressive energy brings peace and productivity. Tasks flow smoothly, and business or work efforts gain momentum. Financial prospects improve with potential for gains or profits. Spend meaningful time with loved ones – connection and gratitude will magnify the month's positive vibration.

SNAKE

A lively, fast-moving month filled with opportunity and celebration. Work may feel demanding due to tight timelines, but productivity remains high. Social engagements and festive gatherings lift your spirits and expand your circle. Financial energy is intense but requires discipline to avoid overspending. Prioritise self-care and moderation to maintain vitality through this exciting phase.

12 | DECEMBER 2026

The Fire Horse Year

10
Thursday

Animal: **Earth Horse**
Flying Star: **3**
Good Day: **Goat**
Bad Day: **Rat**

11
Friday

Animal: **Earth Goat**
Flying Star: **2**
Good Day: **Horse**
Bad Day: **Ox**

12
Saturday

Animal: **Metal Monkey**
Flying Star: **1**
Good Day: **Snake**
Bad Day: **Tiger**

13
Sunday

Animal: **Metal Rooster**
Flying Star: **9**
Good Day: **Dragon**
Bad Day: **Rabbit**

14
Monday

Animal: **Water Dog**
Flying Star: **8**
Good Day: **Rabbit**
Bad Day: **Dragon**

15
Tuesday

Animal: **Water Pig**
Flying Star: **7**
Good Day: **Tiger**
Bad Day: **Snake**

16
Wednesday

Animal: **Wood Rat**
Flying Star: **6**
Good Day: **Ox**
Bad Day: **Horse**

HORSE

As the year draws to a close, energy speeds up once again. You may feel anxious to plan, but don't let impatience cloud your clarity. Reflect on what you've achieved and use this time to set fresh intentions. Financially, prosperity continues, with potential bonuses or extra income. Enjoy the festive atmosphere while staying mindful of rest and reflection.

GOAT

Supportive energy continues as the year draws to a close. Life feels full and festive, filled with joyful gatherings and meaningful connections. Financial prospects remain strong, with possible bonuses or new opportunities for gain. Protect your energy by maintaining healthy routines amid the celebrations – rest and balance will prepare you for the new year ahead.

MONKEY

A dynamic month with mixed influences that require conscious balance. Multiple responsibilities may pull your attention in different directions, so maintain structure and avoid overextending yourself. Financial decisions should be made carefully and without haste. Prioritise self-care, good rest, and grounding practices to stay balanced and effective.

ROOSTER

A fulfilling and successful close to the year. Most Roosters will feel proud of their accomplishments and ready for new beginnings. Tie up loose ends, complete unfinished work, and prepare for the next phase of growth. Relationships remain harmonious and supportive, surrounding you with joy and gratitude as the year draws to a close.

DOG

The year concludes on a high note, filled with optimism and fulfilment. Momentum is on your side – finish projects confidently and celebrate your achievements. Financial energy is auspicious, making this an excellent time for long-term planning and securing stability for the year ahead. Gratitude and reflection will attract continued blessings.

PIG

As the year nears completion, fulfilment and satisfaction take centre stage. Your hard work throughout the year brings tangible rewards. Finances strengthen, and family life glows with laughter, warmth, and connection. Rest will rejuvenate your energy – music, creativity, and joyful gatherings will nourish your spirit beautifully.

12 | DECEMBER 2026

The Fire Horse Year

17
Thursday
Animal: **Wood Ox**
Flying Star: **5**
Good Day: **Rat**
Bad Day: **Goat**

18
Friday
Animal: **Fire Tiger**
Flying Star: **4**
Good Day: **Pig**
Bad Day: **Monkey**

19
Saturday
Animal: **Fire Rabbit**
Flying Star: **3**
Good Day: **Dog**
Bad Day: **Rooster**

20
Sunday
Animal: **Earth Dragon**
Flying Star: **2**
Good Day: **Rooster**
Bad Day: **Dog**

21
Monday
Animal: **Earth Snake**
Flying Star: **1**
Good Day: **Monkey**
Bad Day: **Pig**

22
Tuesday
Animal: **Metal Horse**
Flying Star: **9/1**
Good Day: **Goat**
Bad Day: **Rat**

23
Wednesday
Animal: **Metal Goat**
Flying Star: **2**
Good Day: **Horse**
Bad Day: **Ox**

IDEAL KITCHEN PLACEMENT IN FENG SHUI

In feng shui, the kitchen is often considered an inauspicious area due to potentially harmful energy generated during activities such as cutting vegetables and meat, washing, and accumulating garbage before disposal. Despite this, kitchens play a crucial role, as strategically placing them in less auspicious locations can help mitigate any potential negative influences in those sectors.

It is essential to avoid placing the kitchen in sectors where it might obstruct access to positive energy. When buying a new home or undertaking renovations, it is advisable to position the kitchen in less favourable areas of the house.

IMPORTANT: Kitchens should never be located in the Northwest (NW) sector, as it signifies 'Fire At Heaven's Gate,' which can harm the Patriarch. Adhering to this principle is a fundamental rule in feng shui.

Optimal Kitchen Locations Based on House-Facing Direction:

House Facing	Optimal Kitchen Locations
North:	SW, W, NE
Northeast:	E, SE, S, N
East:	NE, W, SW
Southeast:	W, NE, SW
South:	SW, NE, W
Southwest:	S, N, E, SE
West:	SE, E, N, S
Northwest:	N, S, SW, E

Kitchen placement should align with the house-facing direction. Remember, the one rule that must not be broken is never locating the kitchen in the NW sector.

12 | DECEMBER 2026

The Fire Horse Year

24 Thursday
Animal: **Water Monkey**
Flying Star: **3**
Good Day: **Snake**
Bad Day: **Tiger**

✈️ 🏠

25 Friday
Animal: **Water Rooster**
Flying Star: **4**
Good Day: **Dragon**
Bad Day: **Rabbit**

💆 ❤️

26 Saturday
Animal: **Wood Dog**
Flying Star: **5**
Good Day: **Rabbit**
Bad Day: **Dragon**

⚡ 🪙

27 Sunday
Animal: **Wood Pig**
Flying Star: **6**
Good Day: **Tiger**
Bad Day: **Snake**

🎬 ✈️ 🏠

28 Monday
Animal: **Fire Rat**
Flying Star: **7**
Good Day: **Ox**
Bad Day: **Horse**

29 Tuesday
Animal: **Fire Ox**
Flying Star: **8**
Good Day: **Rat**
Bad Day: **Goat**

💅 🎬 🎉 🪙 ✈️ 🏠

30 Wednesday
Animal: **Fire Tiger**
Flying Star: **9**
Good Day: **Pig**
Bad Day: **Monkey**

🪙

12 | DECEMBER 2026

The Fire Horse Year

31 Thursday
Animal: **Fire Rabbit**
Flying Star: **1**
Good Day: **Dog**
Bad Day: **Rooster**

1 Friday
Animal: **Metal Dragon**
Flying Star: **2**
Good Day: **Rooster**
Bad Day: **Dog**

2 Saturday
Animal: **Metal Snake**
Flying Star: **3**
Good Day: **Monkey**
Bad Day: **Pig**

3 Sunday
Animal: **Water Horse**
Flying Star: **4**
Good Day: **Goat**
Bad Day: **Rat**

4 Monday
Animal: **Water Goat**
Flying Star: **5**
Good Day: **Horse**
Bad Day: **Ox**

5 Tuesday
Animal: **Wood Monkey**
Flying Star: **6**
Good Day: **Snake**
Bad Day: **Tiger**

7 Thursday
Animal: **Fire Dog**
Flying Star: **8**
Good Day: **Rabbit**
Bad Day: **Dragon**

JANUARY MONTHLY 2027 CHINESE ZODIAC OVERVIEW

RAT

A beautifully smooth transition into the next lunar year. You'll feel more centred and optimistic about the road ahead. Take time to celebrate how far you've come and set powerful intentions for the coming Year of the Fire Horse's successor – the Year of the Ox. Reflection now plants the seeds for future success.

OX

The year concludes on a powerful and eventful note. As you step into the Yin Fire Goat year, thoughtful reflection will help shape your direction for the months ahead. Financial prospects remain favourable, but balance your responsibilities carefully – others may lean on your strength and wisdom. Protect your vitality, and you'll enter the new cycle with confidence and grace.

TIGER

As the Fire Horse year comes to a close, reflection brings wisdom and gratitude. Celebrate your achievements and lessons learned – your creativity and optimism will be at a high. Life begins to flow with renewed ease, preparing you to enter the Yin Fire Goat year feeling inspired, balanced, and ready for fresh beginnings.

RABBIT

As the Fire Horse year concludes, you can look back with satisfaction and gratitude. You've grown through action, reflection, and perseverance. Moving into the Yin Fire Goat year brings gentle optimism and continued opportunities for advancement. Absorb the supportive energy around you and enter the new cycle with confidence and open-hearted enthusiasm.

DRAGON

The year concludes on a high note, as strong, supportive energy carries you into the Yin Fire Goat year. Life may feel busy, but rewarding—use this momentum to structure long-term planning. Financially, this is a prosperous period if handled with care. Maintain health, stay grounded, and embrace the Goat year with confidence and optimism.

SNAKE

As the Fire Horse year draws to a close, the energy transitions toward new beginnings under the coming Yin Fire Goat. Professional and social life remain active, and finances stay steady. Use this auspicious time to reflect, reset, and plan your next steps with clarity. Enter the new lunar year with confidence, gratitude, and a renewed sense of purpose.

HORSE

As your ruling Fire Horse year completes its cycle, pause to acknowledge how much you've grown. The lessons, challenges, and breakthroughs of this powerful year have prepared you for a new era of harmony under the Yin Fire Goat. Set new goals with renewed clarity and purpose. This is your time to realign, reset, and ride gracefully into your next chapter.

GOAT

As the Fire Horse year completes its vibrant cycle, take time to realign your vision and reset your intentions. Work matters may intensify briefly, but focus on finishing outstanding tasks rather than starting new ventures. Once responsibilities are wrapped up, allow yourself to relax and welcome the fresh, auspicious energy of the Yin Fire Goat year with open arms and renewed clarity.

MONKEY

A strong and inspiring start to the new cycle. Confidence, clarity, and vitality return, empowering you to move forward with renewed enthusiasm. Work, finances, and relationships all show supportive energy and potential for growth. Harness this vibrant momentum to set meaningful goals and step boldly into the Yin Fire Goat year – your time to shine and build lasting success.

ROOSTER

A fresh start dawns, filled with promise and stability. This is an ideal month to reflect on lessons learned and set clear intentions for the Yin Fire Goat year ahead. Ventures initiated now carry long-term potential. Financial flow remains steady, supporting your ambitions. Approach the new lunar year with optimism, grace, and renewed vision.

DOG

A gentle and restorative month welcomes you into the new lunar cycle. Reflect on your journey with pride and appreciation – you've grown through both effort and experience. The Yin Fire Goat year ushers in nurturing energy, bringing opportunities for personal renewal, stronger bonds, and creative expansion. Take time to rejuvenate, realign, and embrace the fresh possibilities before you.

PIG

The new lunar year approaches with calm optimism and renewal. You step into the Yin Fire Goat year with serenity, gratitude, and confidence. Opportunities for growth and harmony will continue to unfold. Emotionally, this is a time to flow with change rather than resist it – trust your journey and let life's gentle rhythm guide you forward with ease.

JANUARY 2027, Flying Star 6: A Radiant Beacon of Authority and Fortune

January ushers in the illustrious Flying Star 6, a celestial force that brings the energies of authority, power, wealth, and heavenly luck. This star is a harbinger of prosperous times, orchestrating a grand symphony of career opportunities and the realisation of long-held ambitions. Under its glowing influence, one can expect an infusion of enhanced power, elevated status, and the radiant aura of a commendable reputation. As an emissary of prosperity, Flying Star 6 bestows divine favour upon its beneficiaries, particularly those seeking career advancement and success. Middle-aged men, middle sons, and those born under the Rat zodiac sign are especially poised to reap the rewards of this star's benevolent influence.

The veneration of Flying Star 6's positive attributes can establish a commanding presence, symbolising elevated status and influential sway within professional and social circles. Its energetic current encapsulates the essence of authority, empowering individuals to step into leadership roles and distinction.

To fully awaken the potential of Flying Star 6, one must infuse it with vibrant Yang energy. This can be achieved through the harmonious interplay of water features, resonant sounds, and lively activities. Traditional enhancers, steeped in symbolism, can amplify this star's auspicious energies—whether through the dignified presence of a Horse figurine, the subtle charm of Six Gold Coins suspended from a tassel, or the enduring symbol of Gold Ingots.

However, despite its brilliance, caution is advised. External negative influences can unexpectedly cast shadows over Flying Star 6, turning its blessings into turbulent challenges. Such disruptions may manifest as sudden upheavals, abrupt changes, or even kidney or leg complications.

As Flying Star 6 radiates its potent energies, embracing its power with wisdom and awareness can lead to prosperity, authority, and enduring success.

In 2025, the North sector of the Luo Shu or Bagua School of Feng Shui will be graced by the annual Flying Star 7, a key influence on career and business fortune.

The Water element governs the North, and to bolster this sector for optimal career and business success, it is essential to harmonise the Water energy with Metal elements. Enhance the North with metallic colours such as white, silver, gold, pewter, bronze, and black tones to support and balance the Water energy. Incorporate metal décor objects with blue-black accents, and consider adding water-themed pictures or decorative elements to amplify the positive influence. Additionally, placing a Black Tortoise or Dragon Tortoise in this area can further strengthen career prospects and business growth.

Refer to page 12 for this month flying star chart

01 | JANUARY 2027

The Fire Horse Year

8 Friday
Animal: **Fire Pig**
Flying Star: **9**
Good Day: **Tiger**
Bad Day: **Snake**

9 Saturday
Animal: **Earth Rat**
Flying Star: **1**
Good Day: **Ox**
Bad Day: **Horse**

10 Sunday
Animal: **Earth Ox**
Flying Star: **2**
Good Day: **Rat**
Bad Day: **Goat**

11 Monday
Animal: **Metal Tiger**
Flying Star: **3**
Good Day: **Pig**
Bad Day: **Monkey**

12 Tuesday
Animal: **Metal Rabbit**
Flying Star: **4**
Good Day: **Dog**
Bad Day: **Rooster**

13 Wednesday
Animal: **Water Dragon**
Flying Star: **5**
Good Day: **Rooster**
Bad Day: **Dog**

14 Thursday
Animal: **Water Snake**
Flying Star: **6**
Good Day: **Monkey**
Bad Day: **Pig**

ZODIAC SECRET FRIENDS

Zodiac Astrological allies work and play well together, but forming a close bond with your secret friend can bring exceptional luck. Your secret friend holds special significance, and being mindful of this connection can create various types of fortune in your life, whether in work, friendships, or personal relationships.

- **Rat and Ox: Luck of Harmony**

The Rat and Ox share a naturally harmonious bond marked by balance and understanding. Their relationship, built on a foundation of trust and mutual respect, thrives with a sense of security and reassurance. In love, their connection is steady and supportive, fostering a deep emotional bond.

- **Tiger and Pig: Brings a Secret Friend**

When the Tiger and Pig unite, they attract a secret friend who offers unexpected support and guidance. This special ally brings security and comfort, enhancing their relationship with a deep sense of emotional connection and warmth. In romance, this bond creates a profound understanding and a nurturing environment.

- **Dog and Rabbit: Attracts Unexpected Windfalls**

The Dog and Rabbit pairing is exceptionally lucky for attracting unexpected windfalls, whether in financial gains or new opportunities. Their love life is filled with surprises, keeping the relationship fresh and exciting.

- **Goat and Horse: Luck of Helpful People**

Together, the Goat and Horse attract helpful individuals who offer support, mentorship, or resources. In love, this connection benefits from strong support networks, creating a stable, nurturing environment for their relationship to grow.

- **Snake and Monkey: Gambling and Speculative Luck**

The Snake and Monkey thrive in speculative ventures, using their combined intuition and strategic thinking. In love, their relationship is an adventurous journey, filled with excitement and intrigue. They navigate the highs and lows of their romantic journey with a sense of engagement and curiosity.

- **Rooster and Dragon: Bringing Friends and Allies**

When the Rooster and Dragon team up, they attract loyal friends and allies, strengthening their social and professional circles. This vibrant social life enhances their romantic connection, creating a lively, loving atmosphere.

01 | JANUARY 2027

The Fire Horse Year

15 Friday
Animal: **Wood Horse**
Flying Star: **7**
Good Day: **Goat**
Bad Day: **Rat**

16 Saturday
Animal: **Wood Goat**
Flying Star: **8**
Good Day: **Horse**
Bad Day: **Ox**

17 Sunday
Animal: **Fire Monkey**
Flying Star: **9**
Good Day: **Snake**
Bad Day: **Tiger**

18 Monday
Animal: **Fire Rooster**
Flying Star: **1**
Good Day: **Dragon**
Bad Day: **Rabbit**

19 Tuesday
Animal: **Earth Dog**
Flying Star: **2**
Good Day: **Rabbit**
Bad Day: **Dragon**

20 Wednesday
Animal: **Earth Pig**
Flying Star: **3**
Good Day: **Tiger**
Bad Day: **Snake**

21 Thursday
Animal: **Metal Rat**
Flying Star: **4**
Good Day: **Ox**
Bad Day: **Horse**

Using Your Kua Number to Tap Into Opportunities & Possibilities

A Micro Feng Shui Guide for Your Home & Workspace

Your **Kua Number** is one of the most powerful personal tools in Feng Shui. It reveals your **four most supportive directions** and your **four challenging ones**, allowing you to align your environment with the energy that best enhances your life. Even minor, micro-level adjustments—such as the direction you face, where you sit, or how you position your bed—can dramatically influence your luck, clarity, wellbeing, and outcomes.

To find your Kua Number, refer to **pages 154-159** of this planner.

How to Use Your Kua Number in Your Home

Once you know your Kua Number, you can immediately begin to align your surroundings for success. Each Kua direction corresponds to a specific life sector or palace—representing a different aspect of your personal Feng Shui DNA.

Step 1. Choose Your Power Position (Micro Changes That Matter)

- **Sleeping:** Position your bed so your head faces one of your favourable directions.
- **Working:** Sit facing a supportive direction for productivity, clarity, and recognition.
- **Thinking & Planning:** Use your most auspicious direction for decision-making, goal setting, and brainstorming.
- **Relaxing & Self-Care:** Align with your nurturing direction to restore your energy and emotional balance.

These adjustments do not require moving homes—just understanding where to place yourself within the home you already have.

Step 2. Understand Your Feng Shui DNA - The Eight Life Kua Sectors

Your Kua Number links you to eight specific sectors. Four are **supportive**, helping you grow and thrive; four are **challenging**, helping you evolve through lessons and awareness.

Use this guide to identify which directions to activate and which to soften.

SUPPORTIVE SECTORS - Your Four Auspicious Directions

Sheng Qi – CREATION & WEALTH PALACE

Wealth opportunities, authority, success, creativity, reputation, ambition.

Use for work, business, negotiations, launches, wealth-building strategies, and career decisions.

Tien Yi – HEALTH & WELLBEING PALACE

Vitality, well-being, support from noble people, mentors, and teachers.

01 | JANUARY 2027

The Fire Horse Year

22 Friday
Animal: **Metal Ox**
Flying Star: **5**
Good Day: **Rat**
Bad Day: **Goat**

23 Saturday
Animal: **Water Tiger**
Flying Star: **6**
Good Day: **Pig**
Bad Day: **Monkey**

24 Sunday
Animal: **Water Rabbit**
Flying Star: **7**
Good Day: **Dog**
Bad Day: **Rooster**

25 Monday
Animal: **Wood Dragon**
Flying Star: **8**
Good Day: **Rooster**
Bad Day: **Dog**

26 Tuesday
Animal: **Wood Snake**
Flying Star: **9**
Good Day: **Monkey**
Bad Day: **Pig**

27 Wednesday
Animal: **Fire Horse**
Flying Star: **1**
Good Day: **Goat**
Bad Day: **Rat**

28 Thursday
Animal: **Fire Goat**
Flying Star: **2**
Good Day: **Horse**
Bad Day: **Ox**

Use for healing, recovery, self-care, meditation, and daily renewal.

Nien Yen – SOCIAL & CHARISMA PALACE

Love, relationships, networking, communication, harmony, connection.

Use for romance, family time, friendships, social events, and relationship-building activities.

Fu Wei – IDENTITY PALACE

Self-confidence, clarity, decision-making, self-image, inner strength.

Use for study, reflection, spiritual work, planning, and personal alignment.

CHALLENGING SECTORS – Your Four Growth Directions

Ho Hai – ADVENTURE PALACE

Surprises, uneasiness, disunity, minor setbacks, spontaneous change.

Use when you need fresh ideas, breakthroughs, reinvention, or adventure.

Wu Kwei – SPIRITUAL PALACE

Spiritual awakening, inner world, mystical insight, dreams, subconscious.

Great for meditation, journaling, intuitive work—but avoid for significant decisions.

Lui Sha – LIKEABILITY PALACE

Passion, seduction, attraction, charisma, but also disputes or legal matters.

Use cautiously—can enhance romance and charm but may stir emotional intensity.

Chueh Ming – TRIAL & TRIBULATION PALACE

Challenges, karmic lessons, health issues, and misfortune can be activated too strongly.

Avoid using for essential tasks; ideal for storage or quiet, unused spaces.

Step 3. Bringing It All Together

By aligning your body, desk, bed, and activities with your most supportive Kua sector and directions, you:

- ✓ Activate personal opportunities
- ✓ Strengthen your health
- ✓ Enhance love and connection
- ✓ Boost success and recognition
- ✓ Reduce stress and obstacles
- ✓ Navigate life with clarity and purpose

Your Kua Number is your **Feng Shui DNA**—a personalised blueprint that helps you make the most of your environment, one micro-placement at a time.

12 | DECEMBER 2026

The Fire Horse Year

29
Friday

Animal: **Earth Monkey**
Flying Star: **3**
Good Day: **Snake**
Bad Day: **Tiger**

30
Saturday

Animal: **Earth Rooster**
Flying Star: **4**
Good Day: **Dragon**
Bad Day: **Rabbit**

31
Sunday

Animal: **Metal Dog**
Flying Star: **5**
Good Day: **Rabbit**
Bad Day: **Dragon**

Your Kua Number

YEAR OF BIRTH	ANIMAL SIGN	HEAVENLY STEM	BORN BETWEEN...	MEN	WOMEN
1900	Rat	Metal	Jan 31, 1900-Feb 18, 1901	1	5
1901	Ox	Metal	Feb 19,1901 - Feb 7, 1902	9	6
1902	Tiger	Water	Feb 8, 1902-Jan 28, 1903	8	7
1903	Rabbit	Water	Jan 29,1903-Feb 28, 1904	7	8
1904	Dragon	Wood	Feb 16,1904- Feb 3,1905	6	9
1905	Snake	Wood	Feb 4, 1905-Jan 24, 1906	5	1
1906	Horse	Fire	Jan 25,1906-Feb 12,1907	4	2
1907	Goat	Fire	Feb 13, 1907- Feb 1, 1908	3	3
1908	Monkey	Earth	Feb 2,1908-Jan 21, 1909	2	4
1909	Rooster	Earth	Jan 22,1909- Feb 9,1910	1	5
1910	Dog	Metal	Feb 10, 1910-Jan 29,1911	9	6
1911	Pig	Metal	Jan 30,1911 - Feb 17,1912	8	7
1912	Rat	Water	Feb 18, 1912-Feb 5, 1913	7	8
1913	Ox	Water	Feb 6, 1913-Jan 25, 1914	6	9
1914	Tiger	Wood	Jan 26,1914- Feb 13, 1915	5	1
1915	Rabbit	Wood	Feb 14,1915-Feb 2,1916	4	2
1916	Dragon	Fire	Feb 3,1916-Jan 22,1917	3	3
1917	Snake	Fire	Jan 23, 1917- Feb 10, 1918	2	4
1918	Horse	Earth	Feb 11,1918-Jan 31, 1919	1	5
1919	Goat	Earth	Feb 1,1919-Feb 19, 1920	9	6
1920	Monkey	Metal	Feb 20, 1920-Feb 7, 1921	8	7
1921	Rooster	Metal	Feb 8,1921 - Jan 27, 1922	7	8
1922	Dog	Water	Jan 28, 1922-Feb 15, 1923	6	9
1923	Pig	Water	Feb 16,1923- Feb 4, 1924	5	1
1924	Rat	Wood	Feb 5, 1924-Jan 23, 1925	4	2
1925	Ox	Wood	Jan 24, 1925- Feb 12, 1926	3	3
1926	Tiger	Fire	Feb 13,1926- Feb 1,1927	2	4
1927	Rabbit	Fire	Feb 2, 1927-Jan 22, 1928	1	5

YEAR OF BIRTH	ANIMAL SIGN	HEAVENLY STEM	BORN BETWEEN...	MEN	WOMEN
1928	Dragon	Earth	Jan 23,1928- Feb 9, 1929	9	6
1929	Snake	Earth	Feb 10,1929 - Jan 29,1930	8	7
1930	Horse	Metal	Jan 30,1930- Feb 16 1931	7	8
1931	Goat	Metal	Feb 17,1931 - Feb 5, 1932	6	9
1932	Monkey	Water	Feb 6, 1932-Jan 25,1933	5	1
1933	Rooster	Water	Jan 26, 1933-Feb 13, 1934	4	2
1934	Dog	Wood	Feb 14,1934- Feb 3,1935	3	3
1935	Pig	Wood	Feb 4, 1935-Jan 23, 1936	2	4
1936	Rat	Fire	Jan 24, 1936- Feb 10,1937	1	5
1937	Ox	Fire	Feb 11,1937-Jan 30,1938	9	6
1938	Tiger	Earth	Jan 31,1938-Feb 18, 1939	8	7
1939	Rabbit	Earth	Feb 19, 1939- Feb 7, 1940	7	8
1940	Dragon	Metal	Feb 8, 1940-Jan 26, 1941	6	9
1941	Snake	Metal	Jan 27, 1941 - Feb 14, 1942	5	1
1942	Horse	Water	Feb 15, 1942 - Feb 4,1943	4	2
1943	Goat	Water	Feb 5, 1943-Jan 24, 1944	3	3
1944	Monkey	Wood	Jan 25,1944-Feb 12,1945	2	4
1945	Rooster	Wood	Feb 13, 1945 - Feb 1, 1946	1	5
1946	Dog	Fire	Feb 2, 1946-Jan 21, 1947	9	6
1947	Pig	Fire	Jan 22, 1947-Feb 9, 1948	8	7
1948	Rat	Earth	Feb 10, 1948-Jan 28, 1949	7	8
1949	Ox	Earth	Jan 29, 1949-Feb 16, 1950	6	9
1950	Tiger	Metal	Feb 17 1950- Feb 5,1951	5	1
1951	Rabbit	Metal	Feb 6, 1951 - Jan 26 1952	4	2
1952	Dragon	Water	Jan 27,1952 - Feb 13,1953	3	3
1953	Snake	Water	Feb 14, 1953- Feb 2, 1954	2	4
1954	Horse	Wood	Feb 3, 1954-Jan 23, 1955	1	5
1955	Goat	Wood	Jan 24, 1955-Feb 11, 1956	9	6
1956	Monkey	Fire	Feb 12,1956-Jan 30, 1957	8	7
1957	Rooster	Fire	Jan 31, 1957-Feb 17, 1958	7	8
1958	Dog	Earth	Feb 18, 1958-Feb 7 1959	6	9
1959	Pig	Earth	Feb 8, 1959-Jan 27, 1960	5	1

YEAR OF BIRTH	ANIMAL SIGN	HEAVENLY STEM	BORN BETWEEN...	MEN	WOMEN
1960	Rat	Metal	Jan 28, 1960 - Feb 14, 1961	4	2
1961	Ox	Metal	Feb 15, 1961 - Feb 4, 1962	3	3
1962	Tiger	Water	Feb 5, 1962 - Jan 24, 1963	2	4
1963	Rabbit	Water	Jan 25, 1963- Feb 12 1964	1	5
1964	Dragon	Wood	Feb 13, 1964-Feb 1,1965	9	6
1965	Snake	Wood	Feb 2, 1965-Jan 20, 1966	8	7
1966	Horse	Fire	Jan 21,1966-Feb 8,1967	7	8
1967	Goat	Fire	Feb 9,1967-Jan 29,1968	6	9
1968	Monkey	Earth	Jan 30, 1968-Feb 16, 1969	5	1
1969	Rooster	Earth	Feb 17, 1969-Feb 5, 1970	4	2
1970	Dog	Metal	Feb 6, 1970-Jan 26,1971	3	3
1971	Pig	Metal	Jan 27, 1971 - Feb 14, 1972	2	4
1972	Rat	Water	Feb 15, 1972-Feb 2, 1973	1	5
1973	Ox	Water	Feb 3, 1973-Jan 22, 1974	9	6
1974	Tiger	Wood	Jan 23, 1974-Feb 10, 1975	8	7
1975	Rabbit	Wood	Feb 11, 1975 - Jan 30, 1976	7	8
1976	Dragon	Fire	Jan 31, 1976-Feb 17 1977	6	9
1977	Snake	Fire	Feb 18,1977- Feb 6, 1978	5	1
1978	Horse	Earth	Feb 7, 1978 - Jan 27, 1979	4	2
1979	Goat	Earth	Jan 28, 1979 - Feb 15, 1980	3	3
1980	Monkey	Metal	Feb 16, 1980- Feb 4, 1981	2	4
1981	Rooster	Metal	Feb 5, 1981 - Jan 24, 1982	1	5
1982	Dog	Water	Jan 25, 1982-Feb12, 1983	9	6
1983	Pig	Water	Feb 13,1983- Feb 1,1984	8	7
1984	Rat	Wood	Feb 2,1984- Feb 19, 1985	7	8
1985	Ox	Wood	Feb 20, 1985-Feb 8, 1986	6	9
1986	Tiger	Fire	Feb 9, 1986-Jan 28, 1987	5	1
1987	Rabbit	Fire	Jan 29, 1987- Feb 16, 1988	4	2
1988	Dragon	Earth	Feb 17, 1988- Feb 5, 1989	3	3
1989	Snake	Earth	Feb 6, 1989-Jan 26, 1990	2	4
1990	Horse	Metal	Jan 27,1990 - Feb 14,1991	1	5
1991	Goat	Metal	Feb 15, 1991 - Feb 3, 1992	9	6

YEAR OF BIRTH	ANIMAL SIGN	HEAVENLY STEM	BORN BETWEEN...	MEN	WOMEN
1992	Monkey	Water	Feb 4, 1992-Jan 22, 1993	8	7
1993	Rooster	Water	Jan 23,1993 - Feb 9, 1994	7	8
1994	Dog	Wood	Feb 10, 1994-Jan 30, 1995	6	9
1995	Pig	Wood	Jan 31, 1995-Feb 18, 1996	5	1
1996	Rat	Fire	Feb 19, 1996 - Feb 6, 1997	4	2
1997	Ox	Fire	Feb 7, 1997 - Jan 27, 1998	3	3
1998	Tiger	Earth	Jan 28, 1998 - Feb 15,1999	2	4
1999	Rabbit	Earth	Feb 16, 1999-Feb 4, 2000	1	5
2000	Dragon	Metal	Feb 5, 2000 - Jan 23, 2001	9	6
2001	Snake	Metal	Jan 24, 2001 - Feb 11,2002	8	7
2002	Horse	Water	Feb 12, 2002-Jan 31,2003	7	8
2003	Goat	Water	Feb 1,2003 - Jan 21,2004	6	9
2004	Monkey	Wood	Jan 22, 2004 - Feb 8, 2005	5	1
2005	Rooster	Wood	Feb 9, 2005 - Jan 28, 2006	4	2
2006	Dog	Fire	Jan 29, 2006-Feb 17 2007	3	3
2007	Pig	Fire	Feb 18, 2007 - Feb 6, 2008	2	4
2008	Rat	Earth	Feb 7 2008 - Jan 25, 2009	1	5
2009	Ox	Earth	Jan 26, 2009 - Feb 13, 2010	9	6
2010	Tiger	Metal	Feb 14, 2010-Feb 2, 2011	8	7
2011	Rabbit	Metal	Feb 3, 2011 - Jan 22, 2012	7	8
2012	Dragon	Water	Jan 23, 2012-Feb 9, 2013	6	9
2013	Snake	Water	Feb 10, 2013-Jan 30, 2014	5	1
2014	Horse	Wood	Jan 31,2014-Feb 18, 2015	4	2
2015	Goat	Wood	Feb 19, 2015-Feb 7, 2016	3	3
2016	Monkey	Fire	Feb 8, 2016-Jan 27,2017	2	4
2017	Rooster	Fire	Jan 28, 2017-Feb 15, 2018	1	5
2018	Dog	Earth	Feb 16, 2018-Feb 4, 2019	9	6
2019	Pig	Earth	Feb 5, 2019 - Jan 24, 2020	8	7
2020	Rat	Metal	Jan 25, 2020 - Feb 11,2021	7	8
2021	Ox	Metal	Feb 12, 2021 - Jan 31,2022	6	9
2022	Tiger	Water	Feb 1,2022-Jan 21,2023	5	1
2023	Rabbit	Water	Jan 22, 2023 - Feb 9, 2024	4	2

YEAR OF BIRTH	ANIMAL SIGN	HEAVENLY STEM	BORN BETWEEN...	MEN	WOMEN
2024	Dragon	Wood	Feb 10, 2024-Jan 28, 2025	3	3
2025	Snake	Wood	Jan 29, 2025-Feb 16, 2026	2	4
2026	Horse	Fire	Feb 17, 2026 - Feb 5, 2027	1	5
2027	Goat	Fire	Feb 6, 2027 - Jan 25, 2028	9	6
2028	Monkey	Earth	Jan 26, 2028 - Feb 12, 2029	8	7
2029	Rooster	Earth	Feb 13, 2029-Feb 2, 2030	7	8
2030	Dog	Metal	Feb 3, 2030 - Jan 22, 2031	6	9
2031	Pig	Metal	Jan 23, 2031 - Feb 10, 2032	5	1
2032	Rat	Water	Feb 11, 2032-Jan 30, 2033	4	2
2033	Ox	Water	Jan 31, 2033- Feb 18, 2034	3	3
2034	Tiger	Wood	Feb 19, 2034 - Feb 7 2035	2	4
2035	Rabbit	Wood	Feb 8, 2035 - Jan 27, 2036	1	5
2036	Dragon	Fire	Jan 28, 2036 - Feb 14, 2037	9	6
2037	Snake	Fire	Feb 15, 2037- Feb 3, 2038	8	7
2038	Horse	Earth	Feb 4, 2038 - Jan 23, 2039	7	8
2039	Goat	Earth	Jan 24, 2039 - Feb 11, 2040	6	9
2040	Monkey	Metal	Feb 12, 2040-Jan 31, 2041	5	1
2041	Rooster	Metal	Feb 1, 2041 - Jan 21, 2042	4	2
2042	Dog	Water	Jan 22, 2042 - Feb 9, 2043	3	3
2043	Pig	Water	Feb 10, 2043-Jan 29, 2044	2	4
2044	Rat	Wood	Jan 30, 2044-Feb 16, 2045	1	5
2045	Ox	Wood	Feb 17 2045 - Feb 5, 2046	9	6
2046	Tiger	Fire	Feb 6, 2046 - Jan 25, 2047	8	7
2047	Rabbit	Fire	Jan 26, 2047 - Feb 13, 2048	7	8
2048	Dragon	Earth	Feb 14, 2048 - Feb 1, 2049	6	9
2049	Snake	Earth	Feb 2, 2049 - Jan 22, 2050	5	1
2050	Horse	Metal	Jan 23, 2050 - Feb 11, 2051	4	2
2051	Goat	Metal	Feb 12, 2051 - Jan 31, 2052	3	3
2052	Monkey	Water	Feb 1, 2052-Feb 18, 2053	2	4
2053	Rooster	Water	Feb 19, 2053 - Feb 7, 2054	1	5
2054	Dog	Wood	Feb 8, 2054 - Jan 27, 2055	9	6

Auspicious and Inauspicious Directions Based on your Kua Number

Position yourself in a favourble orientation for significant activities. Whether seating a deal, engaging in work or meals, delivering a presentation, attending a learning session, or even during sleep, ensure your head is directed towards a positive angle. Steer clear of unfavourable orientations whenever possible.

Auspicious Directions:

Kua Number	Sheng Chi (Best Direction)	Tien Yi (Health Direction)	Nien Yen (Romance Direction)	Fu Wei (Personal Growth Direction)
1	Southeast	East	South	North
2	Northeast	West	Northwest	Southwest
3	South	North	Southeast	East
4	North	South	East	Southeast
6	West	Northeast	Southwest	Northwest
7	Northwest	Southwest	Northeast	West
8	Southwest	Northwest	West	Northeast
9	East	Southeast	North	South

Inauspicious Directions:

Kua Number	Ho Hai (Unlucky)	Wu Kwei (Five Ghosts)	Lui Sha (Six Killings)	Chueh Ming (Total Loss)
1	West	Northeast	Northwest	Southwest
2	East	Southeast	South	North
3	Southwest	Northwest	Northeast	West
4	Northwest	Southwest	West	Northeast
6	Southeast	East	North	South
7	North	South	Southeast	East
8	South	North	East	Southeast
9	Northeast	West	Southwest	Northwest

2026

JANUARY
MO		5	12	19	26
TU		6	13	20	27
WE		7	14	21	28
TH	1	8	15	22	29
FR	2	9	16	23	30
SA	3	10	17	24	31
SU	4	11	18	25	

FEBRUARY
MO		2	9	16	23
TU		3	10	17	24
WE		4	11	18	25
TH		5	12	19	26
FR		6	13	20	27
SA		7	14	21	28
SU	1	8	15	22	

MARCH
MO	30	2	9	16	23
TU	31	3	10	17	24
WE		4	11	18	25
TH		5	12	19	26
FR		6	13	20	27
SA		7	14	21	28
SU	1	8	15	22	29

APRIL
MO		6	13	20	27
TU		7	14	21	28
WE	1	8	15	22	29
TH	2	9	16	23	30
FR	3	10	17	24	
SA	4	11	18	25	
SU	5	12	19	26	

MAY
MO		4	11	18	25
TU		5	12	19	26
WE		6	13	20	27
TH		7	14	21	28
FR	1	8	15	22	29
SA	2	9	16	23	30
SU	3	10	17	24	31

JUNE
MO	1	8	15	22	29
TU	2	9	16	23	30
WE	3	10	17	24	
TH	4	11	18	25	
FR	5	12	19	26	
SA	6	13	20	27	
SU	7	14	21	28	

JULY
MO		6	13	20	27
TU		7	14	21	28
WE	1	8	15	22	29
TH	2	9	16	23	30
FR	3	10	17	24	31
SA	4	11	18	25	
SU	5	12	19	26	

AUGUST
MO	31	3	10	17	24
TU		4	11	18	25
WE		5	12	19	26
TH		6	13	20	27
FR		7	14	21	28
SA	1	8	15	22	29
SU	2	9	16	23	30

SEPTEMBER
MO		7	14	21	28
TU	1	8	15	22	29
WE	2	9	16	23	30
TH	3	10	17	24	
FR	4	11	18	25	
SA	5	12	19	26	
SU	6	13	20	27	

OCTOBER
MO		5	12	19	26
TU		6	13	20	27
WE		7	14	21	28
TH	1	8	15	22	29
FR	2	9	16	23	30
SA	3	10	17	24	31
SU	4	11	18	25	

NOVEMBER
MO	30	2	9	16	23
TU		3	10	17	24
WE		4	11	18	25
TH		5	12	19	26
FR		6	13	20	27
SA		7	14	21	28
SU	1	8	15	22	29

DECEMBER
MO		7	14	21	28
TU	1	8	15	22	29
WE	2	9	16	23	30
TH	3	10	17	24	31
FR	4	11	18	25	
SA	5	12	19	26	
SU	6	13	20	27	

2027

JANUARY
MO		4	11	18	25
TU		5	12	19	26
WE		6	13	20	27
TH		7	14	21	28
FR	1	8	15	22	29
SA	2	9	16	23	30
SU	3	10	17	24	31

FEBRUARY
MO	1	8	15	22
TU	2	9	16	23
WE	3	10	17	24
TH	4	11	18	25
FR	5	12	19	26
SA	6	13	20	27
SU	7	14	21	28

MARCH
MO	1	8	15	22	29
TU	2	9	16	23	30
WE	3	10	17	24	31
TH	4	11	18	25	
FR	5	12	19	26	
SA	6	13	20	27	
SU	7	14	21	28	

APRIL
MO		5	12	19	26
TU		6	13	20	27
WE		7	14	21	28
TH	1	8	15	22	29
FR	2	9	16	23	30
SA	3	10	17	24	
SU	4	11	18	25	

MAY
MO	31	3	10	17	24
TU		4	11	18	25
WE		5	12	19	26
TH		6	13	20	27
FR		7	14	21	28
SA	1	8	15	22	29
SU	2	9	16	23	30

JUNE
MO		7	14	21	28
TU	1	8	15	22	29
WE	2	9	16	23	30
TH	3	10	17	24	
FR	4	11	18	25	
SA	5	12	19	26	
SU	6	13	20	27	

JULY
MO		5	12	19	26
TU		6	13	20	27
WE		7	14	21	28
TH	1	8	15	22	29
FR	2	9	16	23	30
SA	3	10	17	24	31
SU	4	11	18	25	

AUGUST
MO	30	2	9	16	23
TU	31	3	10	17	24
WE		4	11	18	25
TH		5	12	19	26
FR		6	13	20	27
SA		7	14	21	28
SU	1	8	15	22	29

SEPTEMBER
MO		6	13	20	27
TU		7	14	21	28
WE	1	8	15	22	29
TH	2	9	16	23	30
FR	3	10	17	24	
SA	4	11	18	25	
SU	5	12	19	26	

OCTOBER
MO		4	11	18	25
TU		5	12	19	26
WE		6	13	20	27
TH		7	14	21	28
FR	1	8	15	22	29
SA	2	9	16	23	30
SU	3	10	17	24	31

NOVEMBER
MO	1	8	15	22	29
TU	2	9	16	23	30
WE	3	10	17	24	
TH	4	11	18	25	
FR	5	12	19	26	
SA	6	13	20	27	
SU	7	14	21	28	

DECEMBER
MO		6	13	20	27
TU		7	14	21	28
WE	1	8	15	22	29
TH	2	9	16	23	30
FR	3	10	17	24	31
SA	4	11	18	25	
SU	5	12	19	26	

2026 Year Planner

DAY	JANUARY	FEBRUARY	MARCH
MONDAY			
TUESDAY			
WEDNESDAY			
THURSDAY	1		
FRIDAY	2		
SATURDAY	3		
SUNDAY	4	1	1
MONDAY	5	2	2
TUESDAY	6	3	3
WEDNESDAY	7	4	4
THURSDAY	8	5	5
FRIDAY	9	6	6
SATURDAY	10	7	7
SUNDAY	11	8	8
MONDAY	12	9	9
TUESDAY	13	10	10
WEDNESDAY	14	11	11
THURSDAY	15	12	12
FRIDAY	16	13	13
SATURDAY	17	14	14
SUNDAY	18	15	15
MONDAY	19	16	16
TUESDAY	20	17	17
WEDNESDAY	21	18	18
THURSDAY	22	19	19
FRIDAY	23	20	20
SATURDAY	24	21	21
SUNDAY	25	22	22
MONDAY	26	23	23
TUESDAY	27	24	24
WEDNESDAY	28	25	25
THURSDAY	29	26	26
FRIDAY	30	27	27
SATURDAY	31	28	28
SUNDAY			29
MONDAY			30
TUESDAY			31

2026 Year Planner

APRIL	MAY	JUNE	DAY
		1	MONDAY
		2	TUESDAY
1		3	WEDNESDAY
2		4	THURSDAY
3	1	5	FRIDAY
4	2	6	SATURDAY
5	3	7	SUNDAY
6	4	8	MONDAY
7	5	9	TUESDAY
8	6	10	WEDNESDAY
9	7	11	THURSDAY
10	8	12	FRIDAY
11	9	13	SATURDAY
12	10	14	SUNDAY
13	11	15	MONDAY
14	12	16	TUESDAY
15	13	17	WEDNESDAY
16	14	18	THURSDAY
17	15	19	FRIDAY
18	16	20	SATURDAY
19	17	21	SUNDAY
20	18	22	MONDAY
21	19	23	TUESDAY
22	20	24	WEDNESDAY
23	21	25	THURSDAY
24	22	26	FRIDAY
25	23	27	SATURDAY
26	24	28	SUNDAY
27	25	29	MONDAY
28	26	30	TUESDAY
29	27		WEDNESDAY
30	28		THURSDAY
	29		FRIDAY
	30		SATURDAY
	31		SUNDAY
			MONDAY
			TUESDAY

2026 Year Planner

DAY	JULY	AUGUST	SEPTEMBER
MONDAY			
TUESDAY			1
WEDNESDAY	1		2
THURSDAY	2		3
FRIDAY	3		4
SATURDAY	4	1	5
SUNDAY	5	2	6
MONDAY	6	3	7
TUESDAY	7	4	8
WEDNESDAY	8	5	9
THURSDAY	9	6	10
FRIDAY	10	7	11
SATURDAY	11	8	12
SUNDAY	12	9	13
MONDAY	13	10	14
TUESDAY	14	11	15
WEDNESDAY	15	12	16
THURSDAY	16	13	17
FRIDAY	17	14	18
SATURDAY	18	15	19
SUNDAY	19	16	20
MONDAY	20	17	21
TUESDAY	21	18	22
WEDNESDAY	22	19	23
THURSDAY	23	20	24
FRIDAY	24	21	25
SATURDAY	25	22	26
SUNDAY	26	23	27
MONDAY	27	24	28
TUESDAY	28	25	29
WEDNESDAY	29	26	30
THURSDAY	30	27	
FRIDAY	31	28	
SATURDAY		29	
SUNDAY		30	
MONDAY		31	
TUESDAY			

2026 Year Planner

OCTOBER	NOVEMBER	DECEMBER	DAY
			MONDAY
		1	TUESDAY
		2	WEDNESDAY
1		3	THURSDAY
2		4	FRIDAY
3		5	SATURDAY
4	1	6	SUNDAY
5	2	7	MONDAY
6	3	8	TUESDAY
7	4	9	WEDNESDAY
8	5	10	THURSDAY
9	6	11	FRIDAY
10	7	12	SATURDAY
11	8	13	SUNDAY
12	9	14	MONDAY
13	10	15	TUESDAY
14	11	16	WEDNESDAY
15	12	17	THURSDAY
16	13	18	FRIDAY
17	14	19	SATURDAY
18	15	20	SUNDAY
19	16	21	MONDAY
20	17	22	TUESDAY
21	18	23	WEDNESDAY
22	19	24	THURSDAY
23	20	25	FRIDAY
24	21	26	SATURDAY
25	22	27	SUNDAY
26	23	28	MONDAY
27	24	29	TUESDAY
28	25	30	WEDNESDAY
29	26	31	THURSDAY
30	27		FRIDAY
31	28		SATURDAY
	29		SUNDAY
	30		MONDAY
			TUESDAY

BEGINNERS FENG SHUI
'EASY TIPS TO ENHANCE EVERYDAY LIVING'

Feng Shui, the "art of placement and manipulation of energy".

Embark on a transformative journey into the ancient art of Feng Shui with "Beginners Feng Shui." This guide, meticulously crafted by Michele Castle, distils two decades of expertise into a comprehensive beginner's manual. Uncover the secrets of Chi energy flow and the art of placement to bring balance, harmony, and prosperity to your living space. Whether you're a novice eager to learn or seeking inspiration for your next home renovation, this book is the perfect companion. Delve into health, wealth, relationship, and career strategies through symbolism, placement techniques, and the use of colour. Elevate your understanding of Feng Shui with this insightful guide, ideal for learning enthusiasts and those looking to enhance their homes.

Available Audible, Ebook or hardcover https://amzn.to/3uCoMOU

DISCOVER THE POWER OF PERIOD 9 FENG SHUI AND CHINESE ASTROLOGY 2024 – 2044

Explore the captivating world of Feng Shui and Chinese Astrology with an Audible, Ebook or hardcover copy of "Period 9 Feng Shui and Chinese Astrology 2024 – 2044." Authored by Michele Castle, a dedicated expert in Feng Shui, this book unravels the mystique of Period 9, a twenty-year cycle from February 4, 2024, to February 3, 2044. Discover the transformative power of the Fire Element, fostering personal growth, creativity, and innovation. Delve into tailored Feng Shui techniques, aligning with the energies of Period 9, and envision your dreams becoming reality. Navigate cosmic influences with flying stars charts and dynamic period energy. Join a vibrant community of seekers ready to explore and connect on this enlightening journey. Michele Castle, a trailblazer in Feng Shui, invites you to unlock the secrets of Period 9 for a life-changing odyssey toward unprecedented success and prosperity. For inquiries or courses, contact

michele@completefengshui.com or visit www.completefengshui.com.

Available Audible, Ebook or hardcover https://amzn.to/47AyeRh

www.ingramcontent.com/pod-product-compliance
Lightning Source LLC
Chambersburg PA
CBHW071241070526
44583CB00017B/2277